To JMH
FROM JTH
JUNE, 2014

THE AFI CONSERVATORY

Toni Vellani
on
The Practice of Filmmaking

American Film Institute

THE AFI CONSERVATORY

Toni Vellani
on
The Practice of Filmmaking

Compiled by Gary Winick

Introduction by Bob Gazzale

Forewords by
Jean Picker Firstenberg and James Hindman

Additional Commentary by James Hosney

American Film Institute

Published by
American Film Institute
Los Angeles, California
www.AFI.com

ISBN: 978-0-9899140-0-0

Library of Congress Control Number: 2013949945

Photo of Gary Winick Courtesy of Getty Images for AFI/Kevin Winter
Photo of Toni Vellani Courtesy of AFI
Book design: Future Studio Los Angeles

Manufactured in the United States of America

At AFI
I not only learned the craft of filmmaking but,
more importantly, acquired the courage,
ability and determination
to express myself as a filmmaker.
In doing so, my AFI experience
gave me the tools to tell my stories as a director,
as well as motivated me as a producer
to help other filmmakers tell theirs.

GARY WINICK
AFI Class of 1986

Table of Contents

Introduction

Forewords

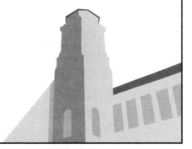

Introduction

by **BOB GAZZALE**
AFI President & CEO
2007-Present

The history of the AFI Conservatory is a proud one, nurtured and grown from seeds planted in the White House Rose Garden by President Lyndon B. Johnson in 1965. It was there and then that were born the ideals of the AFI – to preserve the heritage of cinema, to honor the artists and their work and to educate the next generation of storytellers, "bringing together leading artists of the film industry, outstanding educators and young men and women who wish to pursue this art form as their life's work."

Reflected in those words is one of the most fundamental principles of the Conservatory – that our Fellows should learn by doing, with guidance from great practitioners and established masters of craft.

Proof positive of our commitment to that promise is Toni Vellani, whose collected conversations demonstrate the unique spirit of the Conservatory. Even in the stark black-and-white of the printed page, Toni presents a powerful potion, affecting and immediate –

a formula for creative alchemy and an inspired education about the practice of filmmaking.

This volume represents the last chapter of Toni's time at AFI. It's a story that began when Founding Director George Stevens, Jr., first engaged Toni to inspire the Fellows at Greystone – the original home of what was then known as the Center for Advanced Film Studies. There, Toni influenced generations of aspiring artists, and his wisdom continues to echo even in the halls of AFI's current Hollywood home.

One young storyteller particularly taken with Toni was Gary Winick, a Fellow from the AFI Class of 1986. It is Gary who first compiled Toni's words, and who in turn asked Jean Picker Firstenberg and James Hindman – AFI's leaders for more than 25 years – to put those words into a form for all to share.

These are words which capture what we at the AFI proudly espouse, lessons to celebrate that singular ideal we hold most dear – that story matters.

Foreword

by JEAN PICKER FIRSTENBERG
AFI President & CEO
1980-2007

Gary Winick was a Fellow at the AFI Conservatory in the mid-'80s: someone you remembered
and someone you thought understood what
needed to be done to tell a story well. He, in fact, was
also a visionary – he recognized well before others the
game-changing potential for digital technology for independent filmmaking when he co-founded InDigEnt
(as in Independent Digital Entertainment), and how to
make a movie for under $100,000.

In 1992, Gary sent AFI a letter and a manuscript
he had compiled about his mentor and the AFI
Conservatory's Master Teacher, Antonio Vellani. Gary
had recorded, transcribed and edited comments and
remarks made by Toni in classes, mostly reflecting on
works-in-progress by AFI Fellows. Taken together,
Toni's descriptions of effective techniques go a long
way toward articulating the AFI philosophy on how to
become a cinematic storyteller: "Learn by doing, study
with the masters."

———

Two decades later, Gary died after a long bout with brain cancer. During those 20 years he had made some small movies and some big movies, but he always made good movies. He won awards and recognition, but his greatest accomplishment was his extraordinary capacity to be an amazing friend. His legions of friends can testify to that.

As it happened, just after Gary died, Bob Gazzale, the AFI President and CEO who succeeded me late in 2007, told me they were moving the Institute's central records and files, and asked if I wanted to look through them before they were moved. It was a thoughtful suggestion and one I knew I had to accept. And, of course, this is when I came across Gary's letter and manuscript. It was far more than a coincidence; it was just meant to be.

In fact, Gary had sent the manuscript to James Hindman, AFI Co-Director and COO, and myself, so Jamie was the first person I approached to join in this experience. We had worked together for 24 years at AFI. Jamie was responsible for the evolution and maturation of the AFI Conservatory, and knew Toni well. So, together, this is our effort to bring Gary's ambition to its appropriate publishing place. Together, we asked Bob Gazzale's permission to move forward and meet with Mark Ross, Gary's colleague, executor and close friend to secure his approval and encouragement. Mark did more than that by providing, through Gary's estate, the funding for the design and printing of this book. We also shared the idea with Toni's widow, Sonia, and his daughter, Maria, whose enthusiasm for the endeavor matched our own. As Jamie describes in his comments, we invited James Hosney to be part of this effort. Jim is one of the most superb film historians and teachers we have known and is also a close friend.

Therefore, this entire venture is a collaboration in the best tradition of the AFI Conservatory; even more, it is an enduring testimony to Gary's vision to conceive it. It is his legacy that made it a reality.

A special word to Gary's parents, Penny Williams and Alan Winick. We know your loss is profound, but we hope through this book you will again know how well your son was respected and admired.

Foreword

by JAMES HINDMAN
AFI Co-Director, COO & Provost
1980-2004

This project was envisioned as a tribute to the legacy of the AFI Conservatory, to its philosophy and approach, which have produced generations of remarkable filmmakers over its nearly half-century of practice. The AFI Conservatory was developed at a time when American film education was in its infancy. As the studio system faded, opportunities for mentored professional training had virtually disappeared. The expense and limited availability of production and post-production tools made it extremely difficult for talented and adventuresome young filmmakers to create, experiment, critique and support one another as they learned the best practices of a mature art form.

By the time AFI moved to its new campus in 1981, the Conservatory had become a unique creative environment that took precisely this approach. Young people who were fortunate enough to be admitted came as Institute Fellows – not as students learning at a school, but as filmmakers practicing the art and craft that they

hoped to master, actually making media that aspired
to the highest standards they could reach. And they
would study with the masters, analyzing their work
and discussing it with an illustrious roster of faculty
and guests.

As the Conservatory matured in its new home, it
was Toni Vellani, as Director of the Conservatory and
its Master Teacher until prior to his death in 1989,
who, in the course of his critiques of Fellows' work,
fully articulated the vision, philosophy and pedagogy
that shaped every aspect of the Conservatory program.
Practical details have changed and evolved, but the perspective Toni established has become deeply rooted at
the Conservatory, and its impact continues to be felt at
AFI today.

The impact that Toni had on AFI Fellows, and the
work they would come to make, was truly immense.
As a mentor he was deeply articulate, highly passionate
and remarkably consistent in his approaches to cinema.
One of the Fellows, Gary Winick (AFI Class of 1986),
was so affected by his time with Toni that, after he
graduated, he gathered many months of Toni's recorded
commentaries into a single manuscript. An adroit
compiler, Gary captured Toni's unique, idiosyncratic
voice while distilling and organizing the basic principles
of his critiques and discussions. The result is an
amazingly fresh, quite comprehensive statement on the
fundamentals of narrative cinema.

Vellani was in love with film, especially classic Hollywood film from the golden era. And he had enormous
respect for the creative masters of American and European film. But he had a similar passion for great litera-

ture, classic drama and music. His early training in Law
at the University of Bologna led him to look for logic,
order and fundamental principles in the chaotic world
of filmmaking. As a result, Toni taught the dramaturgy
of cinema, always stressing the foundations and con-
cepts that supported the entire creative process from
script to screen. He believed in the collaborative art
of filmmaking – from the producer and director
to the editor, from the writer to the cinematographer
and designer. Toni was clear in his belief that he was
mentoring filmmakers, and that every member of the
creative team deserved that title.

Yet there was nothing esoteric or precious in Toni's
approach – he believed that filmmaking was a very
practical art. But ultimately it was to the audience that
he always returned, because it was there that the filmmakers' responsibilities finally lay. To move them, to
surprise them, to make them care – no detail was too
small or inconsequential. And Toni would hammer the
filmmakers in his critiques until the film worked for an
audience.

Toni's commentaries and critiques were originally
done in class discussions of the Fellows' short video
Cycle Projects that drive the First Year curriculum at
the Conservatory – therefore this text was first edited to
leave out these specific references. Rather than risk that
Toni's discussions become too general, we have asked
James Hosney to illustrate the broader points Toni
was making with additional references to the classic
Hollywood films he so loved, an approach we believe
Toni would have taken himself were he still here. Jim
taught with him at the AFI Conservatory over many

years (and continues there to this day), and understood his perspective and his tastes really well.

This book is a labor of love, dedicated not only to Toni's extraordinary legacy but also to the memory of Gary Winick, who cared so deeply about Toni's approach to storytelling. At a time when the art of the moving image is changing so quickly and profoundly, it is especially relevant to look again at the fundamentals as Toni saw them. The art of the storyteller is very much alive at the AFI Conservatory, and Toni would no doubt appreciate and respect how it is still taught there today.

The Filmmaker

Vellani: How do we start to make a film? You have an idea, a great idea. What's next? As filmmakers, what we do is turn this idea – this story – into terms of theatrics. By "terms of theatrics," I mean terms that display action, because that's what we are talking about – action. That's all there is. The performing arts universe is action.

I have an idea for God, and I have an idea for the Devil. "God and the Devil" is an idea and I want to do a drama. I've got to cast God and I've got to cast the Devil. There have to be two folks on screen. There's no way to avoid it. The next question is: What is going to *happen* between God and the Devil? We make selections among the infinite number of issues, ideas and complexities that concern the conflict between God and the Devil. This piece – this scene – will be explicit and lucid and will not be redundant; this other scene is going to be this, and so forth. Then we line these scenes up in a structure that will hold an audience. **[Hosney:** *Toni's ideas on filmmaking are rooted in classical Hollywood Style, an approach that focused on character and plot, shot with an invisible style. Throughout this commentary, I will be expanding on some of Toni's ideas and examples to facilitate his unique voice.*]

★   ★   ★

The filmmaker has a story idea. He says, "Can this idea make a movie, or is it better as something else? Is it better for a news-paper article? Is it better for fiction? Is it better for a documentary? Or is it better for this or that?" This is the most significant decision you have to make! After that you have to apply your knowledge of the craft to find out how the story idea – which is just an idea – can be made and molded so that it will fit this particular medium. Film is a limited medium. There are things you cannot do.

★   ★   ★

What are we doing when we make a movie, or when we stage a play? What we are doing is expressing, inventing, fabricating life. We have an idea in our heads. So what do we do? We are going to invent some figures who will be familiar to an audience and then, on screen, something will happen between those figures. There must be action and conflict.

We invent human beings, we put them up there, and they have to do something. They're going to do something to each other for a reason, love or hate or whatever it is. We are going to invent actions, which will be symbolic of something that an audience can participate in. We are going to do what Aristotle calls an "imitation of life." We are not going to duplicate life because it would be stupid to do that. After all, who needs a duplication of something he's already got? What's the use of that? I'm going to resolve the characters' problems through actions. If I don't see the actions on screen, nothing is going to happen.

★   ★   ★

Give me something! Passion. Your piece must be from a person who is saying, "I have a passion to tell you this." If you're going to tell me a story, you have to have a commitment to the people you invented, who they are and what they are. You must also have curiosity about your characters, compassion for them. Then, through *your* curiosity, through *your* investigation of a particular expression of human nature, the people in the audience will understand what the story is about and perhaps learn something about themselves.

★   ★   ★

You can't like your work too much. People who like their own work don't amount to anything. You've got to challenge your story. How can I make it so that it will be endurable to a normal human being, someone who's not connected with the producer, the director, the writer? Right? How can I make it endurable?

Remember that everything is dull! Every scene that is written is *dull* – no matter who wrote it. If you have written it yourself, it's a given! If Shakespeare wrote it, it's still dull, you see? I've seen dull productions of "Romeo and Juliet" and I've seen sublime productions of "Romeo and Juliet." The people who made it worth watching worked at it. I'll tell you, even *that* play, even *that* dialogue, staged for centuries over and over again, can fall flat if the playmakers take the whole thing for granted. [*To prove Toni's point, watch three very different films based on the play: Franco Zeffirelli's version from 1968; Baz Luhrmann's version from 1996; and Carlo Carlei's version from 2013.*]

I'm gonna give you this piece of advice: *Challenge everything!* I challenge everything, and I hope that that's what you're going to learn by working here. Challenge everything! Every moment, every shot!

There is not one shot that is more paramount than another shot; they are all paramount. Ask yourself: What is in the scene? Whose scene is it? How are we going to film it, from whose point of view? Is this character necessary in the play? Are we wasting money shooting this scene? What am I saying with this scene, why should it be in the picture? And, most essentially, what am I saying with this film? Before you can question anything, as a filmmaker, you

must know what you are saying in the film.
[*Although Alfred Hitchcock always emphasized the visual patterns within a scene, Toni emphasized the breaking down of a scene into all of its components because he wanted Fellows to see every aspect of each scene they write. For Hitchcock, "The screen ought to speak its own language, freshly coined, and it can't do that unless it treats an acted scene as a piece of raw material which must be broken up, taken to bits, before it can be woven into an expressive visual pattern."*]

The Premise

Vellani: Before you go into any piece, you must ask yourself: What is the premise? What are we saying? If the premise is not clear in the beginning, by the end, the audience is going to be totally dissatisfied, no matter what you do. No matter how well acted the piece is, no matter how well photographed it is, they won't get what they expect. And what they expect to get is a certain kind of understanding of the human predicament. Unless you touch upon that, your audience is going to be dissatisfied.

★ ★ ★

A premise will tell you what the story is about. Before you shoot every scene, you must think about it: What is this movie about? I recommend doing this very strongly, because it's hard enough when you're making a half-hour film, but if you're doing a feature-length film, you've really got to focus.

You must find a one-line premise for the whole film. A one-line premise for the film will tell you exactly what happens with every one of the scenes. It will become for you, the overall touchstone for the scenes in the film.

What the movie is about – a simple, one-line premise. Before you stage every scene, you read the scene and then you read the one-liner for the film and that'll tell you what particular point has to be made in the scene. I'm not talking about the dialogue. I'm talking about the subtext. [*The subtext is the unspoken thoughts and motives of the characters — what they really think and believe. For Elia Kazan, subtext was a crucial aspect of directing, for both theater and film. Kazan often discouraged his actors from enunciating every word in every line because he wanted them to find the subtext of the scene. Watch James Dean's scenes with Raymond Massey in EAST OF EDEN; Massey performs in the style of classical Hollywood where the actor must speak every line of the screenplay, but Dean sometimes mumbles his lines, creating a clash between Method acting and classical Hollywood acting that emphasizes the clash between father and son, exactly what Kazan wanted. When Dean has a scene with Julie Harris, there's no clash of acting styles because she too came from the Method.*] You have to figure out a way of working that will allow you to do this. Otherwise, if you start to make a long film, you'll be lost halfway through. A premise will keep you on track.

★   ★   ★

Having a well-established premise will help you avoid writing unnecessary scenes. *Economy is paramount in playwriting.* Economy. Stick to that. When I look at a movie, I always think that it's like a dog in the country. You know when they put dogs on a chain? And on the chain, the dog can go out fifty yards, or twenty yards, or twenty feet, and it cannot go any further. You know what I mean?

But as filmmakers, we often have the feeling, "My God, let's gallop around the path down there!" But we can't, we've got the chain, the chain that holds us back, to write the scenes we *must* write. Not the scenes we would like to write. That is the most central thing. Never forget this.

How do you define which are the scenes that you must write? By keeping in mind what you want to say – that is the premise. When you read a screenplay, always ask yourself: What am I doing here? What is the story? Who are the people I'm dealing with? And *don't* confuse the foreground with the background. Quite often we see movies with great battles – thousands of soldiers going to the left, to the right; guys in green and red are fighting each other, killing each other, and we don't give a damn! We really don't, because all we care about is a little guy somewhere who's telling me whose story it is. And it could be the Little Drummer Boy, as far as I'm concerned, and the background is a huge battle. But the foreground is what I'm interested in. You see? That's the major thing.

This happens in the best pieces. As far as social content is concerned, take a look at THE BICYCLE THIEF. It is a story of a father and son. That's all there is, it's as simple as that. And all of a sudden, you have this landscape, the nation, the time, etc., and the film became famous. A very simple story, father and son. That's all there is to it. But made with precision and concentration. Vittorio De Sica didn't make a film about the background – the war, the landscape, the nation – he made it about the people who are in front of the background.

★ ★ ★

Okay, let me explain *premise* once again. A person wants to make a film about war – the philosophical statement that "war is hell." Okay? War is hell. That means we've got to make a movie with a lot of bodies torn to pieces, young men, women torn by life and war. That will be the look of the picture. Lots of bodies, so on and so forth.

What are we going to do? Are we going to find a hero or a bad man? It depends on your point of view. Pick one. All right, I'll pick. Napoleon – we start him as a young officer, Corsican-born. Not a true Frenchman, but he goes to France. The situation is ripe in the French army for an ambitious young man to climb from lieutenant to captain, from captain to general. We see the progression. He goes up, he goes to war. We do all this stuff. Then finally general is not enough. So he becomes dictator. But dictator's not enough. So he becomes emperor, and then being emperor of France is not enough. He has to be emperor of Germany, emperor of Poland, emperor of Russia!

So he goes to Russia, gets beaten to shreds. All of these bodies and so on and so forth. Snow comes down. We have the Battle of Terracina and all that stuff. Napoleon leaves. Napoleon loses everything – winds up a lonely old man in some tenement. Through all these things we have photographed battles galore, bodies everywhere. And, everybody's happy because we showed that war is hell. But is that the premise of the piece? No.

Ambition leads to destruction. That is the premise of the piece. It has nothing to do with war. Because I can take the same young man, and instead of being Napoleon, he's a little guy who's born in the Bronx, right? He becomes the President of IBM. When he becomes the President of IBM, he loses everything he always wanted. Ambition leads to destruction. Same premise. Completely different statement.

The premise is not IBM is hell. See what I'm saying? It's a different thing, that thrust. That thrust has got nothing to do with the environment in which we deal. It's got nothing to do with anything else. It's got to do with "What does this person want out of life, and will he or she achieve that objective?" [*You can analyze King Vidor's THE CROWD and Billy Wilder's THE APARTMENT as examples of Toni's premise. Both films have male protagonists, working in a corporate environment; each must learn what he really wants to achieve in his life and what he has to do in order to achieve his goals. In fact, Billy Wilder and his production designer, Alexander Trauner, copied (to the best of their abilities) the office set that Vidor used in THE CROWD in order to emphasize the influence of Vidor's film.*]

★   ★   ★

"Romeo and Juliet." The premise: Love is stronger than death. It is the love that drives Juliet, and at the end, when these two people are on stage or on screen, one realizes that the other is dead. POW! – the other kills herself.

Fellow: Philosophical statement – Love is hell.

Vellani: Cynical, very cynical. Philosophical statements have nothing to do with premise. You can have all kinds of stories that share the same premise. "Othello": Jealousy leads to destruction. How many plays have that same premise, but have nothing to do with Cyprus, nothing to do with Othello, and nothing to do with a Moorish general who kills his wife? You can apply the same premise to all kinds of stories, and the stories, obviously, will deal with some kind of social, philosophical statement along the line.

★   ★   ★

What I'm trying to get at here is the difference between premise and philosophical statement. A philosophical statement has to do with ideas. A premise is a statement that we use to help ourselves zero in on an action that *characters* take when placed in a particular situation.

What is drama? Drama is where we invent some individuals, some characters, and we put them on stage and they fight against each other like the bull and the matador. The philosophy of the piece may then come out, through the *action* of the characters. I want to be engaged by the characters as I watch the story, not by the point that's trying to be made. The philosophical statement is what I think about on the way home: I say, "My God, that's what the movie is really about!" Interesting, but in the theatre I'm caught up by the actions of the characters.

We are not at a lecture at the Sorbonne; we are at a movie house. We have asked a lot of people to pay money to sit and watch our efforts – we must move them emotionally, not intellectually. Believe me, that's why they're there.

★   ★   ★

I want to make one point very clear: do
not confuse the premise with the plot.
The premise has absolutely nothing to do
with the plot. Nothing. You can apply the
premise, once you have it, to any story you
wish. If you don't apply a premise to your
story from the beginning of the piece – no
matter how you film it, no matter how long
or short it is – the audience will not reach
an understanding at the end, a catharsis.
Your main characters will not go through
experiences where they learn something
about themselves. And thus we – in the
process of watching them – will not go
through experiences that could possibly
make us understand something about
ourselves.

This is true with the Greek plays, if you
read them, and I suggest you do so if you
haven't already. We've got a lot to learn from
these old boys whose works have lasted two
thousand years. There's a great deal in those
works about the craft of playwriting, and
about human nature. [*In dealing with premise,
Toni often referred to Lajos Egri's excellent book,
THE ART OF DRAMATIC WRITING, which you
might want to read in order to elaborate on this
concept, one crucial to screenwriting.*]

★   ★   ★

Fellow:	What is the major problem with my main character in this piece?
Vellani:	What is the premise of the piece? What are you trying to say?
Fellow:	Involvement leads to isolation?
Vellani:	Involvement leads to isolation?
Fellow:	Yeah, getting involved leads to isolation.
Vellani:	But, the guy is isolated at the beginning of the film. He's never involved. You went nowhere. See what I'm saying?
Fellow:	Yeah, I see what you're saying. I felt that he had to be somebody who had retreated from the world. Part of him wanted to participate, part of him didn't.
Vellani:	He was afraid.
Fellow:	He was afraid.
Vellani:	He was afraid and…
Fellow:	He's afraid and he's shy of the world.
Vellani:	And his relationship with the woman, he's afraid of falling in love.
Fellow:	Yes, I see…Fear leads to isolation.
Vellani:	*There* you got something going. Because now you're dealing with fear and the possibility of overcoming it. The premise is the first thing to find, then you have to find a story that supports the premise – in

dramatic terms. So you have to have an individual who is one way, then he learns something in the process.

But I think it is a little unsatisfactory if you have an individual who is one way, then he has already learned what he has learned, and then he goes through and he learns it again. Then at the end people say, "So what? I already knew it." We didn't go into the core of the man.

We are talking about the elimination of that "so what?" – that terrifying line that comes at the end of some films. You ought to think about those two words every time you have an idea to make a movie. The audience can have an extraordinary cruelty, an enormous lack of compassion for people who make films. They love to say, "so what?" We have to make sure that we establish the character change, and establish it very clearly at the beginning; who this person is and what he becomes.

★   ★   ★

So that's why we talk about premise. What is the premise? We keep on insisting about this thing. The premise clarifies what the story's got to be, who the character is, what's going to happen to him. So we see that. We suffer with the characters. Whether it's a drama or a comedy, it's the same thing. There has to be a crescendo, a climax. We have to know exactly what's going to happen to these people – the core of the play is what we're after and the premise makes sure you get to that. The premise is something, I repeat over and over again, that helps the filmmaker or dramatist keep himself honest.

Drama

Vellani: Drama is a question of decisions. In drama, characters are asked to make decisions, and the audience is present when these decisions are made. The process of facing decisions, of overcoming obstacles, pushes a character to reach a certain point. At that moment we show the nature of the character, what he is about. [*Mike Nichols' THE GRADUATE revolves around the decisions Benjamin Braddock has to make in order to get what he wants. At his homecoming party, a business type whispers the word "plastics" to him. Ultimately, Benjamin must make decisions and act on them in order to avoid becoming part of the world of plastics, the world of his parents and Mrs. Robinson.*]

★   ★   ★

Drama is not the result – drama is the decision-making. The moment to capture in a scene is the decision, not what happens after the decision is made. The President of the United States is declaring war; well, is it interesting when he comes out to make the speech? Of course not. It is more interesting to be in his home when he's deciding whether to do it, when he's being advised; somebody says do it, the other guy says don't do it, it may be a mistake. That's the drama, you see what I'm saying?

★   ★   ★

Drama is not inaction. Drama is the time
before the action. One of the greatest statues
I have ever seen is the *Discobolus.* You know,
the man who throws the discus. The Greeks
knew something about drama. When did
the sculptor catch the man in action? This
athlete who has got a discus in his hand?
Before the throwing! The sculptor totalized
a *moment of rest.* The *Discobolus* has more
drama than any futurist sculpture catching
a man in mid-stride. That is the point. The
same thing happens in drama.

STAGECOACH is one of the greatest
films ever made. We are waiting for this
gunfight at the end. The gunfight is over in
two seconds, but the audience is there for
an hour and twenty-five minutes, waiting
for the gunfight. Because everything leads –
structurally speaking, moment to moment,
scene to scene – up to the gunfight at the
end. [*Even the Indian attack on the stagecoach, in
which the Ringo Kid shows the audience his prow-
ess as a marksman, makes the audience anticipate
the final gun battle, which does not last as long as
the Indian attack.*]

★   ★   ★

Film is an action-oriented medium, and by
action I don't mean a car chasing another
car, or a guy taking out a gun and shooting
someone. By action, we mean psycholog-

ical action. In order to have action, you need to have people who want something and people in conflict with them who want something else. We have to see them making decisions. That's the only way there is.

★   ★   ★

Fellow: I'm just thinking about ORDINARY PEO-PLE, because in that film the major conflict with the characters is with someone who is not there, but there's still an on-screen conflict. For instance, his dead brother is still a key element in the story, even though he's never there.

Vellani: The conflict is not that. The conflict is the mother. The brother is the shadow. The conflict is the mother.

Fellow: Right, but it's been put on the screen.

Vellani: There is this particular mystery that we have to resolve, and the brother is ever-present on the screen even though he's not there. But the conflict is between the mother and son. I think it's a marvelous film in that sense, a very contemporary film.

★   ★   ★

When you dramatize something, whatever it is, you have to lead the characters you've chosen to a very clear conclusion. As Aristotle says, you have to have a moment of self-recognition [the Anagnorisis], otherwise

you haven't got a play. Hamlet realizes
certain realities and then takes action. He
acts too late, so he'll die in the process. But
we as an audience require resolution from
the screen. It is a common denominator in
all dramas. You must drive your *story* to a
conclusion because I, the audience, want to
know what you think. I know what I think,
but I want to know what you think. And
what you think has to come across through
your character's moment of recognition.

★   ★   ★

Identification is the strength of drama.
That's why drama has existed for two thousand years and why it's going to be around
for two thousand more. Through the process
of identification, the audience can be approached indirectly through their association
and participation with the emotional lives
of the characters. We find it very difficult to
find these psychological truths about ourselves in real life. The dramatic form was
invented a long time ago, to give us psychological parables. It is easier for us to get in
touch with ourselves through this form than
to face our souls or psyches naked. That is
why drama exists.

★   ★   ★

I want to bring up another subject here, which has to do with the approach to the audience. How much should the audience know that the character does not know? When you're making a movie, you have to decide. Am I going to make an objective storytelling picture, or a subjective storytelling picture? This has nothing to do with the position of the camera. This has to do with the overall narrative thrust of the piece. Is the audience going to know more than the leading character, or is it going to know as much as the leading character?

If the story is *subjective*, the audience finds out information at the same time as the character. If the story is *objective*, the audience may know more about what goes on than the characters, particularly the main character. You can give us more information by not staying with the main character.

Alfred Hitchcock, who makes suspense movies, is always objective. He's always objective because that is the key to suspense. If the audience does not know more about certain events than the character does, there is no suspense whatsoever. There is surprise. But not suspense. Because *suspense* is based on the audience having knowledge that the main characters don't have. But Hitchcock is very subjective when he *shoots* scenes, they're always shot through somebody's point of view, which is *essential* because there we see the emotion of an actor. [*As Hitchcock said, "I believe in giving the audience all the facts as early as possible."*]

★   ★   ★

In drama, you must avoid non-essential elements; avoid the elements that do not have a direct relationship to the main action. These have to be kept to a minimum! Don't make big issues out of minor points.

I've said this many times, you know, that the whole point of drama – in film – is to photograph and heighten the *moments of decision*. The results of those moments are totally uninteresting, they don't mean a thing. What is interesting to us is to investigate the emotional state of these characters when they are leading into a decision.

Comedy

Vellani: Comedy is the most complex and psychologically difficult form of writing. Ed Wynn, a great comedian, once told me something that I'll never forget. He was a student of comedy, a man who'd been in comedy since vaudeville. He said, "Don't do funny things. Do things funny." You understand the difference? You do things funny, but you don't do funny things – incredible things, things that are not real.

You take a look at Charlie Chaplin. He never does funny things. He's always doing normal things. Every single step of the way, but they're funny. He never does funny things. Chaplin's comedy, all good comedy, is based upon extraordinary reality. [*In describing Katharine Hepburn's problems with playing comedy in BRINGING UP BABY, Howard Hawks said, "I tried to explain to her that the great clowns, Keaton, Chaplin, Lloyd, simply weren't out there making funny faces, they were serious, sad, solemn, and the humor sprang from what happened to them...Cary (Grant) understood this at once, Katie didn't." Hawks brought in Walter Catlett, a veteran comic from the Ziegfeld Follies, who played one of her scenes in the film straight, as Katharine Hepburn, so she could understand how to play her role as Susan. The result: Hepburn created an iconic screwball heroine.*]

The core of comedy goes very deep into the psychology of human beings. Laughter is a dynamic component. But, how do you obtain it? How do you do it? Great comedians have quite often used tragic themes. Let's take a look at Charlie Chaplin: THE GOLD RUSH, CITY LIGHTS. All tragic themes. He makes you laugh your head off. KING OF NEW YORK. Tragic: and he pushes it to comedy. [*Chaplin said, "Cruelty is a basic element in comedy...The audience recognizes it as a farce on life, and they laugh at it in order not to die from it, in order not to weep."*]

Let me remind you, comedy is the most difficult genre there is. The audience has absolutely no compassion for failed comedies! A film director friend of mine once told me, "If we go to see one of my movies, if it's a drama and there is silence, I can believe that everyone is very moved by the picture. When I make a comedy and I don't hear the laughter, I know I've got a flop on my hands."

When we go to see a film or a play, or anything that is intended to be a comedy, and we don't laugh, we are furious. We are really furious! In drama, we have a lot of compassion: the audience will say, "Well, it's really not very good but, you know, we're dealing with major themes, so there is justification." But in comedy, when we go in and we don't laugh, we hate it. We really *hate* it.

For some strange reason, we react this way, and that's why it's such a complicated affair. And that's why there are some people who really dedicate their lives to the *study* of this particular genre. Almost all the film directors who are involved in comedy study the form all of their lives – they know *everything*, they've studied every shot, scene, edit, etc., ever made because comedy is one of the most difficult things to achieve. It's hard.

Rule number one: You have to remember that when you're doing comedy, you must have credibility of motivations. That's *foremost*! Because if the audience has *half* an opportunity to reject you, they will! Immediately! The dramaturgical rules are the same as in drama, only more stringent. You can't afford to make mistakes – ever. Because comedy is very *dramatic*; it's tragedy pushed to a different level. If you push tragedy, you wind up in comedy and farce. [*For example, Ernst Lubitsch sets TO BE OR NOT TO BE in Warsaw during the Nazi invasion of Poland, with Jack Benny playing Joseph Tura, Poland's greatest living actor, at least in his own eyes. There's a running gag in the film involving a Nazi Colonel whose nickname is Concentration Camp Ehrhardt, who declaims, "We'll do the concentrating while the Poles do the camping!" At the film's preview in Westwood, the audience was laughing at all the jokes, until Colonel Ehrhardt describes Joseph Tura's acting ability with an analogy: what he does to Shakespeare, we're doing to Poland. The laughter stopped, but Lubitsch would not cut the line.*]

But it isn't a different story you're telling, it's the same bloody story you're telling, only it's pushed, you see, up to a certain point. And quite often we have stories that are very maudlin to tell, and that's when they become comedies. Because they would be too bloody heavy if you did them as straight drama. The only way to avoid the pitfall of an extraordinarily melodramatic story is to push it into comedic terms. Then the audience will laugh – you give them the *privilege* of laughing at a certain situation. That is the nature of comedy, there is no other! Folks, I want to insist over and over again, little gags don't make comedies, they only make lousy television! Take that for granted, that's the case! And you better put in a laugh track because nobody will laugh otherwise, and nobody does laugh!

★   ★   ★

Nobody laughs on the set of good comedies. Because they're not filming gags. Comedies are hard work, and then when it's up on the screen, the people laugh. If you laugh on the set, you're in trouble. Go back to the screenplay; there's something wrong there.

★   ★   ★

Talking about the mystery of comedy, Charlie Chaplin gave this example: You have a scene, it's in an apartment building on the fifth floor, and this little kid drops a *huge* ice cream cone out of the window. Down below there's this poor little beggar girl, and she's holding her hands out. It's Sunday, and she's waiting for people to give her money because she's starving to death. The ice cream cone falls in her hands. What happens? Nobody laughs. Nobody. It ain't funny.

Same scene, same story. Ice cream falls down, and instead of the little beggar girl there's a big pompous lady with a little poodle. A huge, pompous person with a pompous little dog – the ice cream cone falls – everybody laughs! Why? Why? [*Chaplin believed that comedy was long shot and tragedy was close-up: if you watch a man slip on a banana peel from a distance, it's funny; but if you can see expressions of pain on the man's face, then it's tragedy.*]

W. C. Fields made people laugh by tricking the blind man. He pulled it off – a blind man! Did you ever see that bit [*in IT'S A GIFT, 1934*]? It's extraordinary. How he did it is fantastic: There was a pharmacist, right? He's got a drug store. The door is open onto the sidewalk of a well-traveled street, there is traffic, etc. The store is very close to the intersection, and there's a streetlight there with red, yellow and green.

The pharmacist opens the door, and there's a blind man who comes around the corner. The blind man gets confused and instead of turning right, he turns into the store. The pharmacist is helping a customer and he sees this man coming down the aisle with a cane, upsetting all the boxes, you know. The pharmacist excuses himself from the customer and goes over to very kindly take the blind man back to the street. The pharmacist lets him go and the blind man walks off.

Something happens outside; the blind man gets confused and comes back in the store. You see? Same story – the blind man comes back in, even more confused, does his stuff, starts knocking over a lot of boxes. The pharmacist takes him out again, but this time he does it even better. This time he doesn't just let him go when he's out the door, he goes out twenty yards with him and says, "That's it," and he lets him go.

Something else happens again – three times. The "rule of three," you've heard about the rule of three in comedy? Three times the guy comes back in and this time he's *even more* disruptive than he was before – boxes everywhere. Again, the pharmacist takes him out to the street, doesn't let go after twenty yards – he goes fifty yards – he goes all the way to the corner, where the lights are, he waits for the green and *shoves* the blind man off in the middle of the traffic! The people laugh!

The character *had established a relationship with the audience.* You know what I mean? He went *three times* around, you see. Remember the rule of three! Remember it! It's a very good rule. Three is less than four and less than five, it's *much* less than six! You see what I'm saying? Funny, funnier, top it! But after that one, you've had it, don't repeat it again. It's a temptation to go on, but don't.

★   ★   ★

Fellow 1: Peter Sellers does unbelievable things as Inspector Clouseau!

Vellani: Sellers is always credible in the PINK PAN-THER films. I haven't seen all of them, but they're films that I admire very much. The outrageous moments that are in the picture are totally credible at all times, and the characters are within the truth of their own description. Each of them; the Clouseau character is very clear. Cato is very clear. Everything is very clear. And then they're into a fantastic situation. It's extraordinarily credible.

Peter Sellers always disguises himself. That's his shtick. We know that he always wants to make himself up as something else. And at one point [*in REVENGE OF THE PINK PANTHER, 1978*] he makes himself up as

Toulouse-Lautrec. After he appears dressed as Toulouse-Lautrec, he sings "Thank Heaven for Little Girls." It's fantastic! He's outrageous, but he never does funny things; he does things funny. He does what he does, because he is who he is. It is funny because the situation is pushed. [*Here, Sellers conflates José Ferrer's appearance as Lautrec in John Huston's MOULIN ROUGE, 1952, and Maurice Chevalier's singing "Thank Heaven for Little Girls" in Vincente Minnelli's GIGI, 1958. These would not have been obscure references because both films were still very well known.*]

Fellow 2: But you see, if they were making a movie of this class situation and Peter Sellers walked through that door into the movie here, it would be totally unbelievable and you wouldn't believe it for an instant. But you believe it in the set-up of the thing.

Vellani: I'm not sure if I understand what you're getting at.

Fellow 3: I just think you're misunderstanding each other. What Toni is talking about, I think, is not realism in the sense of the way people actually behave but real within the logic of the characters and the logic of the piece.

Vellani: That's correct. There's no other logic in comedy, except the logic that we set for it. There is no relationship with life. There's no relationship with anything other than an imitation of life that we put on stage, which will have its own logic, if you set it up correctly. [*In Hitchcock's VERTIGO, Gavin Elster's plot to murder his wife makes no logical sense, but once Hitchcock draws you into the world of the film through the long sequence of POV shots, as Jimmy Stewart follows Kim Novak through different areas of San Francisco, you accept the logic of the film — like the logic of a dream.*]

Comedies are based on extraordinary reality. No hanky-panky. That is, no illusions. That's the way it is. The manner in which people will behave will make it either a comedy or a drama. But the situation in both cases has to be real.

DR. STRANGELOVE, for instance, is a good example of a successful black comedy. There's no hanky-panky in that film. They're just pushed a little further so that they become ironic. But all those characters are as real as they come. And at no time does the film director, Stanley Kubrick, let you believe that the story is not real. That's what makes it fun. DR. STRANGELOVE is actually based upon a real person, Werner von Braun. Sellers speaks exactly like von Braun. Stanley Kubrick started from a real situation with a real person, then he pushed it forward a bit. It became irony. It becomes black humor when we deal with subject matters that have a great deal to do with our lives. In DR. STRANGELOVE, a formidable example of black comedy genre, we are talking about the destruction of the world. But it's funny. All of the film's people are based in reality. Then, they are pushed. Comedy comes from that push.

[*As Stanley Kubrick started adapting Peter George's "Red Alert," a very serious novel about the possibility of an accidental nuclear war, the more he tried to write a serious screenplay, the more absurd the situations in the novel seemed: "After all, what could be more absurd than the very idea of two mega-powers willing to wipe out all human life because of an accident, spiced up by political differences that will seem as meaningless to people in a hundred years from now as the theological conflicts of the Middle Ages seem to us today." He then brought in comic novelist Terry Southern to help him create one of the blackest and most brilliant comedies of the sixties, DR. STRANGELOVE OR: HOW I LEARNED TO STOP WORRYING AND LOVE THE BOMB.*]

Character

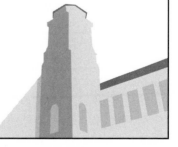

Vellani: I like polite directors. A polite director is one
who treats his film like a party – he invites
you to his house and introduces you to his
friends. When you are at your own home,
and you invite people for dinner, what do
you do when they arrive? They don't know
one another. You introduce them: "Come in
please, Mr. Brown. I would like you to meet
Mr. Gibbons." As a filmmaker, you must
introduce the audience to Mr. Brown and
Mr. Gibbons. You let the audience eavesdrop
on their conversation: Mr. Brown says, "Aha!
Gibbons, finally after ten years I've met you,
eh? You're the guy who screwed around with
my wife ten years ago!" Every story must
begin with a simple introduction.

★   ★   ★

When you're inventing a character, the first
question you have to ask of that character
is: What does he want? That's number one.
And number two: What is his vulnerability?
What does he want and what is his problem?
And then eventually you'll find out the
premise! If you make it a love story, that
means that his love for this woman will get
him out of, or keep him in, the problem he's
got. [*When Hitchcock introduces Jimmy Stewart in
VERTIGO, Stewart and another policeman pursue*

a criminal across the rooftops of San Francisco.
Stewart slips and hangs from the edge of a roof,
and the other policeman tries to pull him up onto
the roof, but falls to his death in his attempt to save
Stewart. In the very next scene, Stewart is trying
to overcome his vertigo, a psychological result of
the policeman's fall. Stewart finally overcomes his
vertigo at the end of the film, but at the cost of
another life.]

★　★　★

CITIZEN KANE. Was that love that he
wanted? That's his story. But he doesn't
understand love. That's why he's a pathetic
figure. That's why he's a dramatic figure.
And then Orson Welles goes more into
depth and you see Kane going through the
motions. The film is very clear. Nobody in
the film knows what Kane really wants –
except the audience. That's the trick.

And the story is that everyone goes
around with an opinion of this man, but
the filmmaker knows the real man, because
the camera goes right down to his essence.
See? That's what we the audience want to
know. We want to know exactly what makes
that man tick. What is driving him? Whether it is to success or destruction, it doesn't
matter. We want to understand that driving
force. [*A newspaper editor sends a reporter,*
Thompson, to interview the people who knew Kane
well in order to find the meaning of "Rosebud,"

Kane's dying word, which he thinks will explain Kane's personality. But Thompson never finds the meaning of "Rosebud," although he comes to the conclusion that no one word can explain a person's life – it's only one piece of the jigsaw puzzle that constitutes a man's existence. Gregg Toland's camera finally reveals the meaning of Rosebud to the audience as it shows Kane's childhood sled, "Rosebud," burning along with many other useless objects Kane has preserved in a warehouse. But Welles earlier signified the complexity of Kane's character when Kane walked in front of a mirror at Xanadu, which reflected his image receding into infinity. At the end, after we see the smoke emanating from the incinerator, we see a sign that reads "No Trespassing," what we and Thompson have been doing throughout the film.]

★   ★   ★

A passive character is going to go down the tubes. He's not going to satisfy us as an audience. He's got to want something, and he's got to take action to get what he wants. We've got to see him fighting for it. And then if he doesn't make the right decisions, we feel for him; we say, "Why do that? It's the wrong thing to do; don't do that!" We get involved. You see what I'm saying? Unless we are privy to the character's decision-making process we are not going to be moved. [*Watch the sequence in THE GRADUATE in which Mrs. Robinson seduces Benjamin; she has to overcome Benjamin's passivity in order to sexually arouse him. Once Benjamin falls in love with Elaine, Mrs. Robinson's daughter, he then becomes active in order to win the object of his desire, actively stealing Elaine from her church wedding after she has married her husband, another "plastic" person.*]

★   ★   ★

The main character in a film is the character that has to make decisions. He or she is the protagonist. The protagonist is the person that is faced with decisions from beginning to end. Either makes 'em or doesn't make 'em. It doesn't matter. That's still a decision. That's your main character.

Your main character is the person who makes, dramatically speaking, the life and death decisions. That's your boy. The other people, the secondary characters, are there to *illuminate* the drama that the main character faces. If you study the great plays, works of literature, etc., you'll find that they contain few secondary characters. The other characters are there for one reason: to help the main character to learn something from his experiences. Zero in on that…don't scatter. The story is about the person who has the decision-making process in his or her hands. [*Michael Corleone develops through his interactions with all of the secondary characters in THE GODFATHER. He first appears as a war hero, wearing his Marine uniform at his sister's wedding; but when he kills the two characters who threaten his father's life, he starts to become a gangster like his father. By the end of the film, he can cold-bloodedly organize the murders of all of his enemies as he's responding to the priest in church at the baptism of Connie's child, in his role as godfather to the child.*]

Whenever you create a cast of characters, make sure that each and every one of them is necessary to the main character's action. If three of your characters are playing the same kind of role, then combine those characters into one. Three characters doing the job of one will not add to the energy of the drama, it will dissipate that energy.

It takes so much effort to introduce a character to the audience; it really does. You have to set him up, you have to cut to a close-up, you've got to tell the audience who he is – first name, last name, his mother, his relationship with this person, that person. If you can cut a character out of the screenplay, do it. If you can combine them, do it; because with each one of them, you have to go through expository scenes to show why the character is there in the first place. What a waste of time if the character is not necessary!

Economy! Economy is the key word in drama. Economy of character, economy of sets, economy of everything. The closer you are to the main character, and his problem, the more the audience will be involved.

Character & Plot

The story is a combination of character and plot. What does this character want? What is his vulnerability? The *plot* is the stuff that we invent to put in the character's path, the obstacles a character faces on his way to getting what he wants. It's a *device* used to show off *what* the character faces on his way to getting what he wants. It's a *device* used to show off the character, the timbre of the individual. Plot doesn't mean a thing. We have seen them all. Not once, but over and over again. How many stories about children who steal? About thieves who kill? How many stories about friendships, about lost lovers who get together at the very end? We have seen them all: there's nothing new. What we are interested in are *the people inside the plot,* people we can identify with.

★   ★   ★

When we make a film we don't really care about the originality of plot. There are no new plots. The plot is part of the story, and many, many times it is the least significant part of the story. Because the plot, as I've repeated over and over again, is devised simply to dramatize the character's dilemma. We have a character who has a goal – a plot is then invented to create obstacles for that character in his movement towards the goal. Therefore, when the character encounters a plot point – which is a jump, like in the steeplechase – we'll find out what kind of timbre that particular character is made of. Picture "The Grand National": You know that a fence is coming, you recognize the fence, it's got a nine-foot fall into mud on the other side. You frame the fence. And when the character reaches that fence, we'll find out what kind of jockey he is!

Remember the business about tragedy and comedy? The Tragic Hero and the Comic Hero may face the same fence… the Tragic Hero had an operation the day before. The doctor advised him, "Don't ride in the National, my boy. If you miss that Number Nine fence, you may die!" And the Tragic Hero says, "I'm the Queen's jockey. The glory is at that fence!" The Tragic Hero will jump the fence and take his chances. The Coward – the Comedic Hero – will try to get out of jumping the bloody fence! But, in the end he will jump it – because he's got a cop behind him.

The plot is a series of obstacles lined up for a character to encounter. The behavior of the character, when he or she encounters the obstacles, will *develop* the character. This *combination* between character development and plot is the *story*. The plot itself is not a story.

We always say that obstacles are critical in drama, as they're critical in acting. But how can I appreciate an obstacle if I don't know what the character wants? You can put all the obstacles in the world in between the character and the obtaining of his goal, but if you don't know what the character's goal is in that scene, what is an obstacle? So, logically speaking, you must tell me what the character wants in order to appreciate the obstacle. Right? A plot is plot. It means nothing.

The story is the psychological maneuvering of these people, in connection with the obstacles that the plot has created. Figure it out and we see who they are. That's why I say, if you just photograph the results, all you're going to photograph is the plot. And in the final analysis this will not be very satisfactory because it won't put us in the position of reaching our catharsis at the end of the piece. We won't feel pity, in Greek terms, and we need to feel *that* for the characters involved, all of them.

★   ★   ★

A thirty-minute film doesn't have to have a subplot, but longer stories, like a two-hour movie, often do need to have one. The subplot, if used, must act as a counterpoint to the primary plot. But, under no circumstances should the subplot be unrelated to the premise of the major plot. Otherwise, you've got two stories. [*Watch Jean Renoir's THE RULES OF THE GAME (1939), in which the plot involving the servants who work in the chateau parallels the plot involving the aristocrats who have come to visit - the two plots tragically intersect at the end of the film.*]

Take a look at any piece of literature. Take a look at "War and Peace." I hate to think of how many characters it's got – but there is not one character in the novel that is superfluous to what Tolstoy wanted to say. All of the characters of that particular work are various aspects – an illumination – of what Tolstoy wanted to convey with that piece. Each one of them.

This is true in plays, as well. Look at every work of Shakespeare. Every single line, every single character in Shakespeare is in there to motivate the action of the protagonist towards the goal. Nothing goes against that idea. Once you know what you want to say, then the subplots and any secondary characters have got to fit in. Otherwise you'll dilute, or even worse, contradict yourself.

Character Development

Fellow: Could you take a specific play and explain
              the psychological action in developing a
              character?

Vellani: Okay. Let's take Shakespeare's "Romeo
              and Juliet." Let's describe Romeo in
              psychological terms. Romeo wants to sleep
              with all the women in Verona, as long as
              they are attractive; he falls in love with a
              different lady every other day. And then, he
              sees Juliet. He says, "I love that girl. When
              she goes to the dance, I'm going to follow
              her."

              "Wait a minute!" his friend says, "The
              dance is over there with this other family;
              they're your enemies!"

              And Romeo says, "I don't give a damn!
              I'm going anyway." What does this tell you?

              It tells you, first, that Romeo is after
              the girls. Second, it tells you that he doesn't
              care about his enemies, he's a reckless man.
              So you're dealing with an individual who's
              emotional and doesn't think much. He
              will not be stopped by a threat to his own
              security. So he's not a cautious man, he's not
              a political man; he's a man who follows his
              emotions.

              Boom! He sees a girl, and he falls in love
              with her, but he does not know who she is.
              That's the beauty of it. When he finds out

who she is, what does he do? He goes to her balcony, a balcony of a house belonging to his enemies! See how it all comes naturally? Because the playwright has set us up. If Romeo goes to the balcony without the psychological setup, without the audience knowing that he's an impulsive man, the audience would say, "I don't believe that Romeo would ever go to Juliet's balcony – the balcony belongs to his enemies."

I mean, the guy's not stupid. You see what I'm saying? The audience would reject the believability and if they don't believe him, the balcony scene goes down the tubes. The playwright says, "I have to make the balcony scene believable. How do I do that? I have to show that Romeo is the kind of guy who would *do* that kind of thing, that it's his character. Aha! How do I explain that it's his character? I'll show him following girls this way and that, with no regard to his reputation or safety." So by the time the balcony scene comes, it's a natural thing and he goes. It's the very thing *this* character *would* do.

★   ★   ★

A character in drama must be *developed*. You go out and photograph an event about a disturbed man who beats somebody in the street. Okay? You take a picture of it. It's fine, it's a piece of news. It goes in the newspaper. But when you're constructing *drama*, that is not enough.

For drama, you have to investigate the reason this particular man does this particular action. It is essential that the character has a goal. What does he want out of life? Did he beat that person to steal? Did he want to feed his family?

Fellow: Maybe he didn't have a reason. Why does he need one?

Vellani: I need one. I need a reason. I am the audience. You have a responsibility to me.

Fellow: But, does it have to be spelled out to you? In life you get to know people like that. That's how they behave.

Vellani: But that doesn't go on stage.

Fellow: Why?

Vellani: What good is it to show an action without a reason behind it? Who cares?

Fellow: But why spell it out? Why not let the audience fill in the reasons themselves? Each member of the audience might have a different, but equally valid explanation for the action.

Vellani: It's not enough! You have to make a statement about life. You are a filmmaker. You fulfill a premise! In order to have a premise, your character must have a goal.

He's got to encounter obstacles to reaching
that goal. And he's got to explain his
behavior in reaching towards the goal.

Fellows! There is no out! Otherwise the
audience is going to get bored! Their time is
wasted! They want to learn something about
themselves when they go to the theatre or
the movies. If you tell me that there are
neurotic people out there, you haven't told
me anything! Do I have to go to the theatre
to discover that? No, because I know it! That
is not enough for the theatre. You have to
explain the logic of neurosis!

★   ★   ★

A crazy man is not interesting dramatically,
unless you get me involved in his sickness. A
schizophrenic world is just a world different
than ours. You see what I'm saying? But it
has its own logic.

I remember in the old days, there
was a very famous James Cagney movie,
WHITE HEAT, about a psychotic killer.
Extraordinary character. Beautifully acted.
And when this man, who's absolutely brutal
in everything he does, dies – the audience
reaches a catharsis. The dramatist had given
a justification for his behavior. And the man
is a killer! [*He dies in a spectacular manner,
on top of a gigantic oil tank that explodes, with
Cagney screaming, "Top of the world, Ma." He's
still psychologically tied to his dead mother, one*

tough broad, not at all a sentimental picture of Mom. Cagney has to show her that he's achieved the dream she had for them, to be on "top of the world."]

★ ★ ★

You have to anchor your characters in reality. It is essential to any story. I've got to know who they are, how they make their money, how they pay the rent, to what class of society they belong. What do they want in life? What is their ambition, and what do they want to have? As a filmmaker you need the empathy of your audience. You need them to want what your character wants. The audience can't want anything for the character if the character wants nothing for himself.

A character can stand for something the audience won't agree with, as long as he stands for something! Have you seen "A Man for All Seasons"? Study that one, folks; that's where it's at.

In "A Man for All Seasons," you have audience sympathy for a character with whom they can't possibly agree. He dies for a reason they cannot possibly agree with. He risks his life throughout the play and finally accepts death rather than the other choice that is given him, for a reason that you cannot possibly agree with in a contemporary world.

If somebody came to you today and
said, "I'm going to write a play, the story
of a man who accepts death rather than
agreeing to a divorce," is it possible that
an audience would participate in this
situation? How can they identify with such
an issue? In drama, the issues don't mean a
goddamned thing. Nothing. "A Man for All
Seasons" is proof of that. It was a marvelous
play and a marvelous film to watch. But
under no circumstances will you ever be
sympathetic to the character's philosophical
point of view.

Fellow: But it was a matter of interest to the nation,
that's why he was in agreement.

Vellani: The nation is not interesting, it's him! The
writer created a character whom you sympathize with because he is who he is. He stands
up for something, which is ridiculously stupid, and at the end, he dies and you suffer.
That's playwriting!

Fellow: But you do agree with his reasons?

Vellani: Under no circumstances do you agree
with him. About the divorce of the King
of England? To protect the Pope, I die?
It's not his reason you sympathize with,
you sympathize with the fact that he *has*
a reason. You see what I'm saying? It's the
man's integrity, not what he stands for!
That's the character – you understand
the difference? You have to understand

the difference between the issue and the
character of the man.

It's the character of the person with
whom we sympathize, not the issue being
debated. You can write a play about
Cromwell that will move an audience.
And Cromwell ordered the decapitation of
Charles the First. The issues involved have
nothing to do with drama.

"The Three Musketeers" – remember the
Three Musketeers, which are four? Who's
the evil man in "The Three Musketeers?"

Fellow: Richelieu.

Vellani: Richelieu! There's a marvelous movie in
which Richelieu is the hero and the audience
dies for Richelieu. [*The 1935 film by Rowland
V. Lee, CARDINAL RICHELIEU.*] It all depends.
Understanding dramaturgy has nothing
to do with the issues, it has to do with the
characters.

★   ★   ★

In drama, we are interested in people who
have deficiencies. We are interested in
people who want to fight their way past
their deficiencies. If they just accept what
they are and they live happily – or unhappily
– ever after, then we are not interested.

But if we see a person who does have
a handicap – whether it's psychological or
physical or moral – and we see them in the

process of fighting against it, then we are
interested! Because your character will be
taking action. If your character is so shy
that he's crippled, if he is *withdrawn* from
society, then we must see him fighting to get
through it!

We want to see him try again. Right?
Something has got to happen. You see what
I mean? In other words, your character has
got to be involved in *action* in order for us
to be involved with him.

★ ★ ★

Don't give me good people on the screen!
I'm tired of them. The interesting characters
are off the wall! They are people who follow
a certain lead, or who are reaching for
something that isn't very good in the first
place. And then in the process of striving,
they are going to find out that whatever
they thought they wanted is not what they
want. They become noble characters because
they are confronted with choices and they
choose. You see?

Nice people are not interesting. They
are not interesting; they are a joke. Just take
a look at the characters in the movies you
remember – they are people that are off the
wall! Otherwise, they're not dramatically
interesting. That's true in literature, in drama
– from the Greeks up to today! Gandhi! Jake
LaMotta! Lawrence of Arabia! They're off the

wall! Otherwise we wouldn't make movies about them. We don't make movies about ourselves because we are boring. I speak for all of us, including myself!

Let's take a look. Was Macbeth off the wall? That's where the drama's at. You see? Take a look at Hamlet. He kills people left and right! He goes through Polonius like there's no tomorrow. He's got a girlfriend, he sends her to Bellevue. She dies a madwoman; he does that to her. You see what I'm saying?

★　★　★

Do *not* be kind with characters! Don't ever make that mistake. You can't be gentle; you learn that from Shakespeare, folks. Push them into a corner, because that's what we want to see. We want to see the dirty clothes washed in public! You know? Otherwise we don't go to the theatre. We go to the theatre and everybody's nice? Well, give me a break; I don't believe it. I don't want to see it. [*In Mike Nichols' film of Edward Albee's WHO'S AFRAID OF VIRGINIA WOOLF? George, Martha, Nick and Honey are not particularly likeable; and the film implies that Nick and Honey might be going home to create their own imaginary child, like the one George and Martha use to hold their marriage together. When George sings to Martha for the final time, "Who's afraid of Virginia Woolf?" Martha replies, "I am,*

George. I am." Is Martha afraid of killing herself, as Virginia Woolf did, because she can't live without her illusions? It's now dawn so there seems to be some hope that George and Martha may survive their night of fun and games with Nick and Honey, however fragile this hope may be. This film works so well because first-time director Mike Nichols and Ernest Lehman, the screenwriter, never tried to soften Albee's characters in order to make them likeable to a film audience.]

★   ★   ★

The best characters in stories are the ones we can turn around one hundred and eighty degrees. That's the best. If you can turn a character around one hundred and eighty degrees, you have achieved something.

In THE BRIDGE ON THE RIVER KWAI, take a look at William Holden's part. When the story starts, Holden steals from corpses, impersonates an officer; he's off the wall. He doesn't do a thing for anybody except himself. At the end he dies a hero. Right? And the other guy, for whom you would die in the beginning [*Alec Guinness' character, Colonel Nicholson, a British officer*], at the end he's a creep. You know? He goes against his nature, consorts with the enemy. In the beginning you would die for him. At the end you want to kill him yourself. That's what makes drama. Paradoxes. Drama is based upon paradoxes! Use them.

★ ★ ★

Do you remember THE APARTMENT
with Jack Lemmon? Take a look at that
character – he's a *pimp*. Beyond belief, an
ass-licker – he'll do anything disgusting, just
to get a promotion. Right? In the process
of receiving the promotion, he realizes it's
not what he wants and chucks it all at the
end. Jack Lemmon plays this part, which
offsets the despicable nature of the character,
but when you study this guy, he's *awful*.
The guy's horrible. [*When Lemmon gives his
boss, Fred MacMurray, the key to the Executive
Washroom instead of the key to his apartment,
he finally becomes a mensch, someone who cares
about and helps his friends and neighbors.*]

★ ★ ★

Take a look at CITIZEN KANE. I mean
Kane does horrible things. But what
compassion is created! This man did not
know what love meant. His mother deserted
him, his father deserted him, and he was
brought up by the bank. So what do you
expect? A man with a heart?

He never had one, but *missed* it. And
all his life he was pursuing it – with this
woman, with another woman, with his
friend, with another friend, with *everybody*.
He misses it. You see how active this
character is? How he is *never* self-indulgent?
He'll go after what he wants. He may make

the wrong decisions, but he will go after his goals, one after the other. That's how we develop a character.

Character Types

Vellani: Say you have a nun who is stuck on a deserted island with another person. This is a rather unattractive nun, who has given herself to the church, you know what I mean? Away from sin. Who is the other person, being male, that I would pick to share this deserted island?

Fellow: Robert Mitchum.

Vellani: No. I choose Don Juan. Not Robert Mitchum, who is an actor. I'd use the real McCoy. Don Juan. Then we've got something going. We've got a nun on a deserted island with Don Juan – you see what I'm saying? Then I know there's going to be some conflict. Right? Don Juan's ability as a seducer will be put to the test, and the nun's Christian faith will also be put to the test. That is what's interesting in a dramatic situation. [*In fact, John Huston sets up this exact situation, but with an attractive nun played by Deborah Kerr and the marine played by Robert Mitchum in HEAVEN KNOWS, MR. ALLISON. They're stranded together on an* *island in the Pacific, held by the Japanese in World War II.*]

★   ★   ★

The innocent is the most difficult part to play. You find very few actors who can get away with it. There used to be Gary Cooper, Jimmy Stewart, Henry Fonda occasionally, when he was young; very few can get away with playing the innocent. If it's not played right, the character becomes stupid.

★   ★   ★

Take a look at Frank Capra's movies. [*Such as MR. DEEDS GOES TO TOWN and MR. SMITH GOES TO WASHINGTON. Both Mr. Smith and Mr. Deeds are innocent idealists; the characters who live by the reality principle become the villains in these films.*] They've got the innocence and they're not stupid. It takes a lot of psychology to pull those things off. And great acting, because the guy has to give, has to have a lot of grace and charm. He can do things because he's innocent, not because he's stupid. Psychologically speaking, this type of character is very difficult.

No character in film can be stupid. That is not acceptable. There must always be intelligence in characters we meet. The theatre and film are not like life. In life, there are a lot of people that are very dumb. Here, in film, there are no dummies. They may act quite dumb, but they have to have a certain amount of intelligence. [*Lucille Ball brilliantly played Lucy in this manner in the TV series, I LOVE LUCY. Ethel was her partner in crime and they often managed to outwit Ricky and Fred. Poor Ricky always needed Lucy to "splain" what she was doing.*]

★   ★   ★

However *introspective* your character may be, if you are making a film about bored people, you cannot use that as an excuse to make a boring film. You have to make an exciting film about people who are bored with life! Otherwise, the audience gets bored, and they get out of the theatre. See what I mean? Character type is no excuse for making an uninvolving film.

★   ★   ★

When you're making a film and an object becomes a character, the *object must become the character.* And people who are acting toward that object have got to act like it's a character. If that chair is a character, and that character is in love with the chair, he makes love to it. You cannot bypass it. That has to be clear.

I remind everyone of 2001: A SPACE ODYSSEY. Do you remember HAL? Of course you do, and that's the point! Kubrick made that machine into a character, and HAL became a being with desires, goals, etc.

HAL's devastatingly horrifying, you know, and the guy became a myth. But why did HAL become a myth? Because Kubrick gave *feelings* to a machine. [*In fact, HAL has more feelings than either of the two astronauts, Frank and Dave, but his emotions cause him to do the horrifying things he does. Dave has to be reborn as the Star Child, a new step in man's evolution, a child who might become a man who can balance his mind and his emotions.*]

★ ★ ★

When you are making a movie about a creative person, whether it is an actor, a painter, or whatever you choose, you have to make the audience know very quickly whether the character is talented or not. Do not think for a second that the actor that you have hired for the part will show that. It doesn't work that way.

We have seen Laurence Olivier playing the part of a bad actor [*in THE ENTERTAINER*]; but the audience knows Laurence Olivier is a great actor. So how does the audience make the distinction? They don't know that Olivier is supposed to be a bad actor. The film has to make the point, so you provide an approval or disapproval within the film.

Let's go back to CITIZEN KANE. When Kane's wife is attempting to sing the opera? How does Orson Welles show that she is a bad singer?

Fellow 1:   The vocal coach is having trouble teaching her, so she's no good.

Vellani: No.

Fellow 2:   Kane builds an opera house.

Vellani: No.

Fellow 3:   It's her performance. The teacher directs her.

Vellani: No.

Fellow 4:   The teacher sings the notes.

Vellani: No.

Fellow 5:   Kane pays the teacher more money.

Vellani: No. You guys see movies all the time, but you haven't watched.

Fellow 6:   Kane pays the reviewers, doesn't he?

Vellani: No. That's after the fact. The camera is on the woman, singing on the stage. The camera tilts up, it goes up and up and up. The camera finds two stagehands up in the rafters who are holding their noses. That's how Welles shows it, loud and clear. And that's how the audience knows the singer stinks. Otherwise they would not know, do you understand what I'm saying? *You have to tell them.* You have to lead them by the nose.

★   ★   ★

In tragedy, the main character must have extraordinarily high moral standards. In comedy it's the opposite. The story can be the same, the same situation, but the character must be different. In tragedy, the main character will find glory at the end, through supreme sacrifice. So the guy at the end will lose his life for his principles, say Thomas More, or some war hero, by blowing up the bridge. In comedy, the character will obtain glory by achieving all of that for the *wrong* reasons. He's trying to run away from the enemy and he accidentally blows up the bridge. And you laugh. The story is the same. So as comedy shows the lower side of human behavior, tragedy must show us the higher side. We need to find the right moral standard for the particular type of story we are working on.

I've said it over and over again. That is the way drama operates. You have a *character* who is after something, all right? On the way, he will find an obstacle or a series of obstacles. Consider that a film or stage play is like a steeplechase – you've got the jumps to go over. The jumps are what the playwright *invents* in order to put that character at the brink of action, of choice. That will allow the audience to find out who the hell he is. How the character reacts to the obstacles, the choices: that's where we see the moral standard of character.

Structure

Theory

Vellani: Structure is the central aspect of filmmaking, and the most difficult thing to learn. It's not as complex as you might think and that's what you have to remember. Don't make it more complex than it is. Don't forget that you are dealing with a medium which is based upon action. Every scene must be written and acted in a fashion that will create emotion in the audience. If a scene doesn't do that, cut it out. Every scene has to lead toward the conclusion. The accumulation of one scene and another scene and another scene will lead to the final crisis so that when you have the final shot the audience will reach a catharsis. It will not be reached unless you build to it. I have nothing further than that statement. There is nothing more to proper structure than that.

★ ★ ★

A film, like a musical performance or a theatrical performance, is connected with time. It's not a single event that you see, like a painting or photograph. It's exactly the opposite. In creative works that have nothing to do with time, it's totally different because in those works, the artists, if you forgive the expression, will seek a moment, a *still* moment of eternity. In other words, they freeze a moment in time and that moment has to give us the suggestion of eternity. And that's when the piece will be called a work of art. Therefore, we watch it and watch it and watch it. And we can watch it over and over again, forever. And we never get bored.

Theatre, film and music are exactly the opposite. They are performing arts. They are locked in time. Whether it's half an hour, an hour, two hours, three hours, four hours – whatever it is, a film is a *connecting of moments over time.* You send information out to the audience, one, then the other, then the other – all within a time structure that the author has chosen. That accumulation of information must add up to something.

To use a mathematical analogy, you go from one to ten, okay? Then you go from eleven to twenty, and so on and so forth, working your way to a hundred. Hopefully, the last shock of the piece will sum up to one hundred and the audience will say, "Aha! I got one hundred." Finally. But, if you fail to let the audience know that the sum and the numbers that you have chosen are 1 to 10, 11, 12, 13, 14, by the time they get to 20, you have lost the audience, because the numbers are just numbers scattered about.

The audience fails to sum up – and finally says, "Don't go see that piece, it's boring."

This process is called structure. We talk about structure all the time and that's what it is: letting the audience know how the sum goes up over time. That is *the* factor in any art that has to do with performance.

The structure of a two-hour piece is completely different from the structure of a three-hour piece. They've got nothing to do with each other; you're in a completely different ball game. The added length will change completely the dynamic of the play.

In films, a lot of people like to break the structure down into acts. I hate that word because it has to do with theatre. I think in terms of movements. I think film has got more to do with music than with anything else. Three movements. The third movement of the piece is called the climactic period. And by climactic period, in dramatic composition, I mean, an area of time where the main character has no decisions to make; he will just act, and we'll know why. In other words, there are no scenes of psychological development in that particular movement. [*Alfred Hitchcock compared film to music when he stated, "I would prefer to write all this down, however tiny and however short the pieces of film are – they should be written down in just the same way a composer writes down those little black dots from which we get beautiful sound."*]

The psychological development usually
occurs in the second movement. If you
insert a scene in the climactic period, which
has to do with the psychology of the main
character, you're doomed. You're down
the tubes, you're boring, you're *finito*. I
have only seen it done once successfully
in cinema. In LAWRENCE OF ARABIA,
there was one scene in the bloody film that
risked for a moment to be a psychological
scene, right? Well, the film director knew
what he was doing. He staged that scene
on camels' backs rather than in a tent as
anybody would have told him to do. He
kept the bloody scene moving. But as you
know, in the second half of that movie, they
are going to go to Damascus. And they are
going to let you know that they are going.
And nothing is holding them back from
Damascus!

Think about a main character as
somebody who is in a submarine. Have
you ever been in a submarine? It's very
claustrophobic, because every time you go
through a door it locks behind you…and
then you go through another door and it
locks behind you and you know you can't
go back, you see what I'm saying? And
there is air there, and you go deeper and
deeper and deeper and deeper. And you have
those locks. And I always imagine the main
character in that climactic period as a person

who just can't go back because he is who he is or she is who she is and that's the way it stands and the person has got to go ahead, even if it means he can never go back.

The best structure in a film that I have ever found is the second version of BEN-HUR. The second version was directed by William Wyler and written by a very famous playwright named Christopher Fry. [*Although Karl Tunberg received sole onscreen writing credit for BEN-HUR, Wyler often acknowledged Fry as the person most responsible for the screenplay.*] Fry designed the whole concept of the picture. No dummy, I assure you. That film is absolutely ironclad from the point of view of structure. Study structure, study that movie. Within three-and-a-half minutes of a very long show – I think it's three-and-a-half-hours long – you know exactly what the play is about, you know exactly what the confrontation is going to be. Then take a look at what happens in the last hour of the film. One climax after another. Ben-Hur with Messala, Jesus crucified, the woman is found, the miracle comes. [*Ben-Hur's mother and sister are found and cured of leprosy after Jesus dies.*] It's relentless. And it's all *designed*. The filmmaker had a plan.

It's essential that there be this kind of design in any creative work that has to do with time. You see? You can't start something and conclude it, then start something else and conclude it and on and on. Because we won't be able to sum it up! The scenes must live individually and not one as a conclusion to another. Okay? All the scenes need to lead to one conclusion or the story becomes episodic where there is no climax. There can be only one story told – *one conclusion* – in each film.

★   ★   ★

When you make a story about two people, don't think you can make a story about two people. You make the story about one of the two and then you end up with the two. You have to make up your mind who is the lead, and stick with him or her. And if the conflict is done correctly, you tell the story of both of them. But not by shifting positions, because then the audience does not know where to be when the story's being told and who to follow. You know, DAYS OF WINE AND ROSES has got one lead, Jack Lemmon, not two. The other character's point of view becomes clear because you follow the path of one of the two. Because if you make a story about two people and you make them both the lead, you'll wind up by telling the story about nobody.

In drama, you have to have a force, and then you have an antagonistic situation; conflict arises and the filmmaker has chosen a character's point of view to tell the story. If the filmmaker shifts the point of view to another character, it is only to support the main character's story. And in the end you have a fully realized relationship about two characters. The audience can strongly identify with either of the characters. [*Or the switch in point of view can make the audience re-evaluate the actions of the main character, as in VERTIGO, when Judy writes the letter to Scotty in the last third of the film, telling him how she and Gavin Elster deceived him in a plot to murder his real wife; now the audience can feel the cruelty of Scotty's actions when he, too, tries to remake Judy into Madeleine.*]

★ ★ ★

Always remember that *film is a snake.* It goes from Beverly Hills to Santa Monica. As long as that, maybe longer. It goes through a machine at a constant speed. It's a piece of celluloid that goes through a machine and it runs at twenty-four frames per second. That speed cannot be altered, it always goes at twenty-four per second. Therefore, changing the rhythm within the film will not come from the machine, but must come from the rhythm that is chosen by you when you're directing or editing. Once a reel hits the machine, it doesn't go backwards. It goes forward. You can't stop, you're in there, you're caught. You're moving forward all the time, forward within the limitation of time. [*If you're directing a comedy, the pacing becomes crucial. Pedro Almodóvar believes, "...another key element in comedy: the rhythm, the timing. Timing in comedy is not like rational time. When the actor gives his reply, he hasn't had the physical or mental time to assimilate the previous line, but he has to deliver his at full speed. No one is going to wonder if he's understood what was being said, and it's a bad sign if a spectator does wonder."*]

★ ★ ★

When you're writing a short story, you've got one point to make and that's it. Not three hundred and fifty. A short story, as opposed to a novel, is usually designed in a fashion where it starts from here and it climbs, climbs and climbs, relentlessly. And then at the end you have one climax. That's a classic form of storytelling in a short story, and it's a classic story structure for feature films. Because both forms lead to the one climax. Which sometimes can be just a line, you see, which turns the whole thing around – obviously in film you can't do it in a line – but the structure – the crescendo – is the same. One story, one climax. Don't structure a film like a novel with many possible stories and many possible climaxes along the way.

Homer's advice? He was a very clever man, Homer was. Great control of how the story's told. Take a look at "The Odyssey."

The whole structure of that piece is a masterpiece. Homer's advice is: *Never repeat yourself.*

The audience can't stand to hear or see the same thing twice. Unless that is the point, like in RASHOMON, where repetition becomes part of the drama. But in most cases, the audience resents repetition, so don't do it!

★ ★ ★

Odysseus wants to go home. You know, Homer says, "I want to go home!" Everyone knows. No questions asked. And you know he's gonna go home. You need to know this. If you don't tell the audience Odysseus wants to go home from the beginning, then by the time you get to the middle you begin to ask yourself, "Where the hell is he going anyway?" You think I'm joking?

That's what the audience does, either psychologically or physically. If they don't know where Odysseus is going, they put the book down – they leave the theatre – they don't care because no end is in sight. If the audience doesn't know where the character wants to go, they won't begin to look for the end. For all they know, the story could be endless. So, why would you stay?

You must tell us at the beginning of the piece! Tell us! What the character – any character you like – wants. The major

thrust of the piece, the whole goal, the
main action, tell us what the protagonist
wants – and then tell us who the antagonist
is, and by God, the audience will be with
the main character. Otherwise you make
things terribly complicated for us because
every time you do a scene, you have to
start anew. You have to be completely
entertaining in every scene because a story
is only a collection of scenes. You gain from
the experience of the previous scenes and
the previous sequences, so the audience can
eventually add it up. If the audience knows
what the character wants, they can begin
to wonder if he will get it. If they begin to
wonder, you got them.

★   ★   ★

A writer should write the scenes that he
must include in the play – not the scenes
he would *like* to include. Don't ever forget
that. If a scene is not necessary for that
piece, throw it away. Or keep it for the
next script. If the scene doesn't fit into the
pattern and path that you have designed
for your film, it must be cut. Economy is
essential! Dumas, the son, asked his father,
"How do you write a play, Papa?" And Papa
replies, "First act clear, third act short, and
exciting all the time." [*Billy Wilder cut Walter
Neff's death scene in the gas chamber at the end
of DOUBLE INDEMNITY; instead, he ends the*

film with Walter collapsing in front of the elevator in the insurance building; we know he's dying because we've been watching the bloodstain on his coat becoming bigger and bigger as he narrates the story of how he came to be wounded. The last scene between Neff and Keyes resolves their friendship and we assume Neff is dying when he collapses - there's no need to show him dying in the gas chamber; because it would be too much - Wilder knows exactly when to end a film.]

You know in films you haven't got much time, you've got to push forward. When you are making a point, there's the next point and the next point that has to be made. The cardinal sin for a film director is to fall in love with a scene! When the filmmaker says, "Jesus, I've got the best dream sequence that was ever devised," you know that the dream sequence is going to be in the picture no matter what: "You can cut everything, but not the dream sequence!" In my experience, that's the first scene to cut. You must think of the whole story – not just that one terrific moment.

★　★　★

Whenever you find a scene that doesn't work, don't watch that scene, watch the scene prior to that. Always remember this. In a film we pay for the sins of our parents. If we become bored in a scene, that means the sins are in the setup, in the scenes preceding the problem. Problems will pile up if you make one bad decision. A film is a sum of its parts. *Every scene* counts. *Every scene* has an effect on the film's conclusion. [*In THE BAD AND THE BEAUTIFUL, the director, von Ellstein, tells the producer, Jonathan Shields, "A picture that's all climaxes is like a necklace without a string. It falls apart. You must build to your big moment and sometimes you must build slowly. To direct a picture a man needs humility. Do you have humility, Mr. Shields?"*]

Technique

A movie is written first, and then it's filmed. The writer and director make a path for the characters to follow; they make a plan of action. It's like a railroad – you get on and you go to the end. If you make a wrong switch along the way, you'll never get to your destination. Remember this when you're on the set and begin to improvise.

Improvisation is terrific and it can be used as a means to do scenes, but it's tricky. On the set, improvisation may be terrific from an actor's point of view, as long as the scene takes you from this point to that point. But if you start mucking around, you wind up with confusion. I've worked with directors who never knew where they were going to put the camera when they went to the set. But they *knew the story* very well and knew exactly what each scene had to say. I don't recommend that beginners try that, but I've seen folks with experience do it well.

The story, the path, the premise has got to be clear first, because you can't change the story in the middle. If that takes place, you're doomed. It's impossible to get back, it's physically impossible. It may happen once in a lifetime, like the man who breaks the bank at Monte Carlo. They advertise the winning for the next 60 years so a lot of suckers will go and spend a lot of money. But it's not going to happen every day.

★ ★ ★

Why use a flashback? Using flashbacks should be forbidden in film schools, because it's like a violin: you've got to know how to play it. I regret that somebody named this narrative device "flashback." A movie goes forward! It doesn't go backwards. So, if we want to engage an audience, narratively, we have to go forward. You can use the flashback only if it propels the story *forward* at a faster speed. Flashbacks *almost* always impede the momentum of a story. There are exceptions, of course, but they are rare. Please, the next time you are at the typewriter [*Read: Computer*] and you're thinking about the scene you're going to write and you have the idea to use a flashback, throw it out! Don't even consider it. Find a more interesting way to get the information out in real time. Flashbacks are too often used as a crutch by lazy filmmakers. Don't fall into that trap. Don't be lazy.

★   ★   ★

If you must use a flashback, be careful to set it up correctly. If you want to say, "Toni is talking to this Fellow, but he's actually thinking about the time he was playing with a goat when he was seven years old," where do you put the camera? You put it on me, because that's where the memory comes from. As I begin to speak, you go closer to me. You see my eyes doing something different because I begin to drift off and think about something else, and then you show the classroom from my point of view. I take a look at the Fellows, getting awfully bored as I'm talking, and you register this in your image. You establish my point of view of the class, and then the class becomes an Italian landscape. You have now conveyed something significant in film terms. See how it works?

In the *script* you write "cut to flashback." But when you film the script, you've got to make it clear to the audience that they're seeing a flashback. You have to establish that it's me who's thinking, then you go back and find the Italian landscape. It takes work to do it correctly. [*In THE ENGLISH PATIENT (1996), Anthony Minghella and his editor, Walter Murch, make the flashbacks crucial to understanding the characters in the film. But they do this in such an intelligent manner that we come to accept the flashbacks as an integral aspect of the telling of the story.*]

★ ★ ★

Some major films have been made using flashbacks. CITIZEN KANE, LAWRENCE OF ARABIA, SUNSET BLVD. and so on, and they work. They work because, in these instances, they are the best way to tell the story. Usually all those devices: flashbacks, voice-overs, etc., do not work well. They become afterthoughts. In SUNSET BLVD., a flashback details the memory of an individual who has reached a certain point in his life. He's taken back and he's telling us about this one remarkably unforgettable incident in his life. [*We first meet Joe Gillis, the narrator of SUN-SET BLVD. as a corpse floating in a swimming pool. He narrates his story so we can understand how he got there. Originally, the film opened in a morgue at night, with the corpses telling each other their stories, before Joe begins his narration. But when they previewed the film, audiences started laughing during this sequence and kept laughing throughout the film. Once Wilder cut that opening sequence*

the film played beautifully with preview audiences.]
It is a major moment for us to know about,
so the voice-over and flashback are the sim-
plest, most economic and precise ways to tell
this story.

★　★　★

You have to assert your authority as a
storyteller. You have to do that at the very
beginning. "I'm going to tell you this tale
in French or in English." Choose your
language and choose your devices. Then,
if they're well done, we won't quarrel with
them. Obviously, you must choose the
narrative style, which is the most exact, the
clearest, the shortest possible way to tell a
specific story. And be consistent.

★　★　★

You have to be very careful using time lapse
in films because the difference between one
scene and the next is *one cut.* A splice. You
have to think in film time because that's the
time you are dealing with. The only thing
that we have in reality that is fixed is time.
We all know that time goes, the clock goes,
and there's nothing to do about it. As soon
as we change that, like we do in films, reality
is down the drain.

You want to do the biography of
Methuselah? His life has lasted what, nine
hundred years? If you make the movie, you

have to fit the life of Methuselah into *hours*. That's the time you're working with, not the nine hundred years. You have to show the passing of nine hundred years in two hours. That's not easy.

★   ★   ★

Setting up the passage of time has always been a problem in drama, whether in theatre or film. It is even more complicated these days, because in film some of the solutions that were found in the past are no longer applicable. Or they're not what we want to see, like *fade-outs* or *dissolves*. Those effects no longer have the same meaning that they had in the past. You've got to be very cautious with those devices.

The best way to go from one scene to the next is a cut. Not a dissolve or a fade – a cut. That means that every scene in the screenplay leads to the next scene with a single cut – no matter how much story has passed. We want to make films that appear seamless. We don't want the audience to see the threading, the needlework of little old ladies in Pasadena. Once we see little old ladies doing the work, the mystery is gone.

Documentaries

Vellani: Let us talk a little about the documentary. It is often said about this type of filmmaking that you should not have structure, should not have precision, and so forth and so on.

I have the opposite point of view. This kind of moviemaking requires more structure and more precision than almost any other type. Because you do not have the control over the situation that you have when you cast and you build the set and create the other elements of a non-documentary film. Therefore, the pre-production and the thinking process that precedes filming must be more rigid and precise than those in a dramatic piece.

Documentaries don't have a length which is prescribed by habit. We go to the theatre on Broadway or we go to see a feature film, and we know it's two hours. An hour and forty-five minutes. Whatever it is. But it's just about that long. A theatrical play's about two hours.

When we see things on television, there is a fixed timeslot. Thirty minutes. Sixty minutes, etc. It's written on it. It's a key piece of information. The audience knows that it's an hour. Two hours.

In documentaries, you don't know how long it may be, okay? If you don't show

it on TV, because there it's written down.
Therefore, the structure is even more
critical, because the structure's the rhythm.
Even the lack of timeframe in which
documentaries are made must tell us where
we are at. [*Frederick Wiseman's LA DANSE is
three hours long, and Claude Lanzmann's SHOAH
is almost nine hours long. But the length of each
film is justified by its subject matter: Wiseman
takes us through the Paris Opera School of Ballet,
showing us various teachers working with their
ballet students, while Lanzmann confronts us with
horrifying testimonies by victims and perpetrators
of the Holocaust.*]

First of all, it is always advisable to have
two things going on at the same time. Since
you have no control over the length of this
one, no control over the length of that one,
what you do is: set up a situation where
you can cut from one to the other. So you
don't bore the hell out of the audience. THE
CHAIR is a classic example, structurally
speaking. You have a person who is con-
demned to death in the electric chair, and
you have the lawyer for the defense, and you
have the prosecutor. Right? So you can stay
with the guy in jail. Then you can go to the
defense attorney, and if he goes on and on
and on, you can always cut! So you have to
create a situation where there are various
forces that move towards an event, in this
case, the verdict. If you want the film tech-

nically correct, correct it technically. So you set up a situation, a structure under which you have some degree of technical control.

Another method used in documentaries is a physical clock that will give an audience a sense of structure. In a dramatic situation you don't need a clock except in certain movies. If you're making an adventure movie, you must have a clock. You've got to tell the audience where the characters are going and when they're gonna get there.

By clock, I mean a time limitation, a deadline, in dramatic terms. In HIGH NOON they put in a real clock. In most cases the clock is the deadline that the protagonist needs to beat. You know – "get the money in two days or your family dies." Adventure stories usually have people going from this point to that point. The deadline adds tension to the trip. But most narrative films don't need that because the rhythm of the scenes themselves and the dramatic structure that is inherent to the piece will lock up into a form where one scene leads to the next, the next scene leads to the next, up to a point that, through the experience of the character, the audience will reach what we call a catharsis.

Adaptations

Vellani: A movie cannot do everything; it can do very little. Begin with that assumption. Begin to understand the limitations of the medium. You've heard it said: "Terrific, I can do everything with movies." That's wrong. Film is a medium that has no imagination whatsoever. You photograph a chair, and it's a chair. If you want to make that chair mean something – for example, my grandfather's chair, the one that he sat in when I was a child, or it's a judge's chair, from which a verdict will soon come – you've got to *show* that the chair has meaning.

Meaning doesn't come from the fact that the chair is photographed, it comes from the chair's place in the structure of the story. The photography means nothing. When you photograph a film you've got a cinematographer, grips, the coffee shop, the honey wagon, and you've got the guy in the chair. What do you do? Lights on the left, lights on the right. You shoot. But, meaning doesn't come from the chair, it comes from the structure of the scenes – the manner in which you put the play in order. [*In THE GODFATHER, Francis Coppola uses Don Corleone's chair in his office as if it were his throne. At the beginning of the film, Don Corleone occupies the chair as if he were born to do so; at the end, when Michael occupies the chair, he doesn't have the grace of Don Corleone — he's playing a role his father never wanted him to play.*]

Many times I've read screenplays by Fellows and they'll have a flashback: "So-and-so as a child" — so they cut to a kid. Well it's a kid. Just another kid picked up from central casting. If you want that child to be the son of somebody who is now thinking about the loss of the child on Thanksgiving Day because the kid is not there anymore, you've got to work at it. If you want the shot of the kid to have emotional force you have to structure the piece so that the audience will know what showing the character as a child, *at this point* in the story, means to the story. All the camera angles in the book will not help you add meaning to a scene if that meaning is not *established first* in the story. [*Orson Welles uses the flashback to Kane's childhood in a most creative manner. When Thompson reads Thatcher's memoirs concerning his first encounter with Kane, the period at the end of a sentence in Thatcher's manuscript becomes a black dot in the snow that transforms into young Charles Foster Kane riding his sled "Rosebud." The lyrical style of this sequence contradicts Thatcher's cold writing style. This day marks the end of Kane's innocence with the loss of his mother — now Thatcher and his bank will become his new parents. Ironically, the first Christmas present Thatcher gives the young Kane is a sled named "Crusader."*]

We have to take "ideas" and turn

them into a form that is acceptable to this
medium. You don't photograph ideas – you
turn them into metaphors. Real metaphors
that can be photographed. The ideas must
be filmable. You cannot write the shot's
intention in the script's stage direction.
The intention, *the meaning*, must be in the
action of the characters, or in their dialogue.
Every "idea" in your script must be filmable,
not simply explained in the stage direction.
For example you cannot write this scene:

```
INT. CHURCH — DAY

The PREACHER reads from his
bible...

                PREACHER
        Do you, Jack, take Jill to
        be your lawfully wedded
        wife?

JACK, nervous for the first time
in his life, answers...

                JACK
                I do.
```

If you write that scene you are not a
filmmaker, you are a novelist writing in
screenplay form. A filmmaker would write:

```
INT. CHURCH — DAY

The PREACHER reads from his
bible...
```

           PREACHER
    Do you, Jack, take Jill to
    be your lawfully wedded
    wife?

JACK, his hands shaking
uncontrollably, answers…

           JACK
      I do.

Do not make the mistake of arguing that any decent actor could play the first scene. An actor can play nervous, but he can't play nervous for the first time in his life. Do you understand that? A novelist can write the first scene and the audience will accept "nervous for the first time" because the audience understands and accepts what it reads. A film audience can only accept what it sees. A film audience cannot read the screenplay. For the film audience to get "nervous for the first time in his life" they must see him say it after the wedding; or better yet, they must see a life of stoic character before the wedding. If you don't understand the distinction between these two scenes, you should not be in this profession. You should be writing books.

That's the first question: Is this material suitable to the screen? Can this piece be translated into a dramatic form or not? Is it better served if we leave it alone as a short story? As a book? The whole language of film is different.

If you do wish to adapt a piece from literature, you have to first think about what moved you in the piece and see to it that you can translate that emotion into film terms. Can the idea of the piece, the emotion, be translated into action? [*Charlie Kaufman and Spike Jonze's ADAPTATION demonstrates what happens when you try to adapt a piece like Susan Orlean's "The Orchid Thief" that doesn't work as a traditional narrative. The last third of the film becomes the sort of bad Hollywood film that results when the writer tries to shoehorn the complex material of "The Orchid Thief" into formulaic story structure — even the film score sounds like that of a typical Hollywood action film.*]

In literature, a writer can explain to you exactly what goes on inside a character's head; one line will do it. But, when you make an adaptation, what happens to that description and the writer's point of view? The *author's* point of view in drama is lost completely; that's a major difference between theatre and literature. In theatre, you don't have an author! We don't give a damn about the author! The only persons we like or dislike, or are emotionally involved with, are the characters that are invented; the author is anonymous.

For years and years and years, people

have been speculating about Shakespeare's identity. The medium of the dramatist is such that we know a great deal about Hamlet but we know very little about the person who created this character. The characters are enormous and the dramatist is in the back. In literature, the author is gigantic. Everything in literature permeates through the author – the style of writing, the commentary, the point of view towards life – that's why we read novels. Novels are for grown-ups. Movies are for children. You know? And I'm not talking about the people who go to see them; I'm talking about the people who make them!

All right? That's the point. I'm making something of a joke out of it, but what I'm pointing out is the difficulty of adaptation. The first thing you have to ask yourself when you do an adaptation is: What am I going to do with the author? Because you may have been seduced by the style of the writing, or by what the author represents. There are authors in the world of literature who are much bigger than their works. They become myths during their lifetime. Voltaire is one. Voltaire's life was much bigger than anything he's written. He was a symbol to the European intelligentsia, of a point of view toward life. When you read and analyze his works, you find out that they fall short of his reputation. You don't adapt literature

into film because of the author's reputation.
You adapt literature into film because the
author's story would make a good movie.
The road to good intentions is paved with
empty theatres.

★ ★ ★

Literature is a much more sophisticated way
of communicating a story than film will
ever be. Because in literature you can shift a
point of view so quickly; you don't have this
garbage to take on – setting up scenes, etc.
You know you can move, in space, in time,
so quickly. You can go forward, backward
and forward with great precision. You can't
do that in film.

When we are transporting a story from
a literary medium to a dramatic medium,
we have to re-think the thing very much, all
along the line. Once the writer's veil – the
descriptions, the *voice* of the author – once
that veil is lifted off, the filter through which
we see the world of the story disappears.

What are you going to do to replace it?
What are you going to do to recreate the
author's voice through filmable action? If
you can't answer that question, don't do the
adaptation.

★ ★ ★

In drama we want motivations. And you'd
be surprised how many short stories by great

writers – that you begin to adapt to drama – don't hold water. And because these authors write very well, especially short stories, they get away with it!

You know, we were involved in making a film a long time ago about a person who was supposed to have murdered somebody, and it wasn't clear in the short story whether he had done it or not. You have to know if the guy killed this person – dramatically speaking. How are you gonna play it? Is he a murderer or is he an innocent person? I mean, what are you gonna do? So we tried to do this and that and finally we called up the author. I got on the telephone and said, "Listen, did he or did he not?" And she said, "Well, I mean, do whatever you wish, really!" You see, that was her answer; she didn't care. And I kept asking her to give us some kind of hint. Finally she said, "Well, I mean, really, you know, you have worked on another one of my pieces and I have complete confidence that you will do great justice to my work," and that was that. I had a feeling she did not like being asked because she had never thought of it. This is not always the case, but this time I think it was.

I'm mentioning this because when you adapt a piece of literature, you no longer have the persona of the writer. And when you're trying to investigate drama, all these things come about. What is the drama, what is the character's motivation? Why does he do this? Why does he do that? You know, with one very simple little line you can get away with it in literature and it doesn't matter. But in film it becomes central because everything we do in this medium demands believability. We must be credible, whether it's comedy, drama, tragedy, whatever you wish. We must believe the character's actions, because that's all we have in this medium: actions. People do things, and we watch them making decisions. One way or the other, decision-making is the lifeblood of drama. Therefore, we want to know why characters do things, and they have to be credible to us.

★ ★ ★

What is the essential difference between film and theatre? Film has one property that the theatre doesn't have. Sometimes we watch a film and complain that it was "theatrical." What do we mean? In theatre, the audience is in a fixed position. You buy a ticket, seat 25, row 11, you sit there for the entire play. You can't change your position, ever. If you try to change seats in the middle of the performance, they're going to throw you out. You take your seat and you see *everything* on stage, all the characters, all the time, from the same point of view.

The difference in film, the real power of

this medium, which I repeat over and over, is that you have the ability to "change the audience's seat." The audience can witness the story from the point of view of any of the protagonists. There is no other secret in this medium. You control what the audience sees. It's magic. Everything else is nothing. Certainly, we do not have the power of presence because we don't have people in the screen. It's a magic art; all you have is illusions. But you have the power to move a person from scene 25 to scene 40, and the audience can witness it from any point of view you choose. You tell the audience what to watch, what matters in a scene. Successful filmmaking depends on how you make these choices – what you decide to show.

★   ★   ★

The adaptation of plays into cinema is very difficult. With a bad play you can say, "I don't like this scene, it's too long, let's cut it out," but with a good play it's harder because it works so well on stage. As you know, it's very difficult to do Shakespeare on film because it's got everything. It's got motion, movement, irony, etc. What you have to do is throw out the play entirely, and just pick up the story. What's the story about? Two lovers. One is like this, the other one like that. Enough. Enough from the play; then you write the screenplay.

Otherwise you wind up with talking heads –
photographs of people talking to each other.

But theatre has in common with film
one thing: it is based upon action and is
supposed to be performed. Theatre's primary
action is dialogue and is usually, for good
plays, very terse, very economic, because it's
the subtext that we are interested in. That's
why actors will try to understand and play
it. In film, we must photograph the subtext
– which is not the dialogue – otherwise the
audience will get bored. [*Shakespeare wrote
all of his plays to be performed; he never wrote
for publication: he acted, directed, and ran his
company. Because he never looked at any of the
published versions of his plays, we have markedly
different versions of some of the plays, such as
"King Lear."*]

A play is a completely different
experience than film. It is meant to be
watched live, with people talking to each
other and interacting with each other; the
experience is completely different from
film watching. In film, you can't rely on
the text of the play. Never think, as I have
heard many times, that to make a movie
out of a play, all we have to do is open it up.
If a filmmaker takes a play and instead of
photographing it on stage, goes to the beach,
it still remains a play. If this is done, then
instead of doing a complete re-evaluation
of the piece, he has taken it outdoors, and

opened it up, changed the set. But if he has merely changed the sets, he should just have followed the play and stayed in the same set. At least then he would have kept the integrity of the piece.

The idea of "opening up" is ridiculously stupid. Because if there is one medium that can go into one set and make that set look like four football fields, it's cinema. For example, I once saw a documentary about ants. They made the ant farm into a world, using the camera. They had long shots, medium shots, close-ups, etc. It was amazing. The Japanese film WOMAN IN THE DUNES was a terrific film with almost no locations. I've seen marvelous films made about men in jail – you see what I mean? Nobody said, "Why don't you open it up?" Well, you can't open it up because the guy's in jail, okay?

In adapting plays into the movies you don't need more sets – you need "less talking and more action." That does not mean you have to cut dialogue and add chase scenes. It means you have to translate a static form of storytelling into a moving form. You have to create emotion from choosing points of view with your camera. [*In HIS GIRL FRIDAY, Howard Hawks and his writers created a new beginning for their adaptation of "The Front Page," a twenty-minute-long opening in a film that runs for only seventy minutes. But it sets up the film in a way the opening of the play would not have done.*]

Any time you decide to pick up a piece of work and translate it into this medium, you have to ask yourselves the one question, "What does this medium contribute to it; why do it?" Unless there are obvious things, you know: you have a great musical on Broadway, so people can't buy expensive theatre tickets, so you give them the opportunity to see SOUTH PACIFIC or THE SOUND OF MUSIC on film. And then you try to do it as cinematically as you can. Then I understand the reason to do it.

But when you don't have a financial motivation or reason behind it, and just really want to do it, I think the major question is: Why is this particular story going to be successful as a film? What in it can be cinematic? Without those little moments of inspiration you're going to wind up with a photographed play. You see? If you keep it the same, it's the same.

Why do it? That's the major question. But if you're doing it, if you like what the play says, then I advise you to forget that it's a play and tell it as if it's an original story that you want to film. Start from the beginning. Ask yourself, "What can film contribute?"

Words are not the strength of film. Beautiful dialogue is *not* its strength. What matters is the action, the photographing of the subtext of that action. That's interesting. But nothing else. [*Hawks also realized the importance of silence in HIS GIRL FRIDAY. He told Rosalind Russell, who was concerned about the amount of dialogue in the film, "You're forgetting the scene you're gonna play with the criminal. It's gonna be so quiet, so silent. You'll just whisper to him, you'll whisper, 'Did you kill that guy?' and your whispering will change the rhythm. But when you're with Grant, we don't change it. You just rivet in on him all the time."*]

Genre

Vellani: I think it's a mistake to say about a film, "The film's made in this genre, I've seen them before." We have seen everything before. You can take any kind of subject matter and either make a bad movie or a good one. [*And some directors question the boundaries between genres. According to Pedro Almodóvar, "...Anglo-Saxon critics are less flexible when it comes to accepting a mix of genres, something as natural in life as it is in cinema. From when you get up in the morning until you go to bed at night, you move through various, sometimes opposing, genres. Since the start of my career that is how I've understood cinematic narrative."*]

You have to remember that THE MALTESE FALCON was made twice before John Huston made his version and nobody has ever seen those other movies. They stink. So, there you go. The same material, the same book, the same everything, but the approach is different.

★　★　★

When you create a world of *science fiction* – as soon as you push a film into that kind of stratosphere – you've got to provide some kind of statement concerning the human predicament, and be very, very clear about it. You can't change human nature, that you know. So the psychology of the characters inhabiting this type of film is exactly like that of the characters in other films. Therefore, the statement that you make on the human predicament has to be clear in this new world, so we know what we are dealing with. Otherwise, we're going to ignore it and resent it.

As soon as you take a story and you project it into the future – a thousand years from today or whatever – you inherit another obligation: What is your vision of this future world? And how are you going to translate that vision onto film? And, therefore, you have to work out the details and know exactly what will happen. What do I eat? How much money do I make? You must think about all of these things, many of which we take for granted.

The audience knows the reality they live in. We know that we can't run an automobile unless we go to the gas station, and we know how much gas costs. In the world of the future you have to tell me all this. What car do I drive? Do I drive at all? Is this smog relevant? You have to create the world. [*Ridley Scott uses every aspect of production design to create the worlds of ALIEN and BLADE RUNNER. In the latter film, there are even porn magazines appropriate to the future portrayed for sale at a newsstand. Although we barely see them, they comprise part of the authenticity of Los Angeles in 2019.*]

And if the social contract among people has changed, you have to tell me; so the film then becomes a philosophical and sociological treatise. And that is what science fiction is all about. All science fiction films are philosophical and sociological treatises which comment on today's world.

George Orwell wrote a book about the future which exposed and analyzed what he thought was wrong with the way the world was moving into the future. So that's what we are talking about. As soon as you go into the future, you've got this obligation. And if you don't answer the obligation, I get bored, because I say, "Well, why set it in the future?"

★   ★   ★

Children's stories have got to be terribly mature! You can't fool around with those, otherwise, we don't read them. Usually, children's stories are horrible! The first time I started reading fables – you know, somebody gave me a book of fables to read for Christmas…and they give you the book, and it has a nice jacket, and you read the stuff – you're terrified! You hate it! You know people *die* and things, they are tormented, they've got to dance forever with red shoes on! You know that Hans Christian Andersen story. You see what I'm saying? We can't stand childish stories about children. All stories about children are very profound so if you haven't got anything to say, folks, don't say anything. Not with children.

★ ★ ★

Fables must be extremely precise. Otherwise, they wouldn't be fables in the first place. They wouldn't survive the centuries if they didn't have, in their extraordinary simplicity, some reach into the depth of human psychology. Don't ever approach a fable saying, "Well, this is a fable. So people don't have to believe it." A fable we believe all the time. We must believe. When you stage them, they must be real and they must be believable, no matter what the story is. Take Cocteau's BEAUTY AND THE BEAST – that beast is real, boy, and she's in there, a beautiful woman, and we believe that they are together.

You remember the one that they did about Dorothy? THE WIZARD OF OZ – and it's perfect! You know, those characters are so deep! They are representations of life with understanding, psychological understanding. That's when fables are fables – when they are absolutely ironclad and perfect. And they'll survive the test of time.

When you're dealing with this genre, that's what you're dealing with. You've got to be grounded, because the audience is going to be terribly critical with you. Much more

than if you do a little drama about somebody killing somebody, whether it's love or
jealousy or whatever. They're going to be
very, very critical. Because they expect that
when you're through, you say something
profound. In an amusing way, in a kind of
nonchalant way, and in a way that is mean-
ingful in some way. But you have to go *very*
deep into human behavior.

★   ★   ★

How do we set up an adventure story, which
involves an attack on a castle, or an escape
story which involves a break-out from a pris-
on, or a caper story about a bank robbery?
The way to do those stories is to make sure
that the details are clear and iron-tight. For
example, in a caper story, there must be a
period prior to the robbery – you've seen
hundreds of these movies, some badly made,
some very well made – where all the members of the gang get together and draw plans.
And they say, "The bank is here – at eight
o'clock you're going to be there with the automobile. Eight-fifteen, the guy goes down
below and then we have to go through this
thing, and we go down that way, then we
drill the hole in there, and by that time it's
ten-thirty, and so on." We set up all of these
points early, and then, during the execution,
we find out the weaknesses of our characters. [*In RIFIFI, THE ITALIAN JOB, THE ASPHALT*

*JUNGLE, THE KILLING and RESERVOIR DOGS, a
character's weakness causes the heist to go awry
or causes the money from the heist to lose its value,
becoming pieces of paper blowing in the wind.*]

★   ★   ★

Every love story has to have a balcony scene.
I assure you, and I repeat this again: You
cannot do a love story without a balcony
scene. I'm referring to ROMEO AND JU-
LIET. There has to be a moment where the
man falls in love with the woman and the
woman falls in love with the man: not in
a carnal sense, mind you. But it's the same
thing, it has to be there. You have to have
the balcony scene! If you take that scene out,
you have no drama. Every love story has to
have, as I said before, a balcony scene.

★   ★   ★

Films dealing with the subconscious have to
be terribly clear, otherwise you're going to
lose the audience. They must have a straight
narrative line that relies on a plot line, even
though the film deals with the subconscious.
Don't believe that you can get away without
it. You have to have that because, as I've
said many times, the plot is a sequence of
obstacles that the protagonist must hurdle in
order to achieve a goal. [*In Alfred Hitchcock's
SPELLBOUND, one of the first Hollywood films to
deal with the subconscious, Gregory Peck goes*

into a fugue state whenever he sees parallel lines. His psychoanalyst, Ingrid Bergman, must uncover the childhood trauma causing Peck's psychological problem. When Peck dreams, we experience a stylized dream sequence with sets designed by Salvador Dali, but Bergman explicates the dream for Peck and the audience. And, of course, when Bergman cures Peck, they fall in love.]

So in works that examine the subconscious, the clarity of exposition and language must be triply clear. A good example of this would be the film 8½. You just take a look at the clarity of the exposition in that film. Everything that goes on is perfectly clear. That is why that movie, occasionally, can take off and go into extraordinary directions. *[In LADY IN THE DARK, Ginger Rogers' sessions with her psychoanalyst and her dreams become big musical production numbers, with songs written by Kurt Weill and Ira Gershwin, all shot in hallucinatory Technicolor. Ironically, in an earlier film, CAREFREE, one of her last films with Fred Astaire, he plays her psychiatrist. Thus, Ginger Rogers stars in the only two classical Hollywood musicals whose plots revolve around psychoanalysis.]*

★ ★ ★

What is surrealism? Here, we are dealing with something deeper than realism. So, it's got to be more real than realism. Because you're touching upon the quintessential meaning of a given situation. If you take a look at the work of Luis Buñuel, it's very bland; there's no trick photography, there is nothing! It's super realism. Except that the whole point of it is as an investigation of the bourgeois society. But the photography, etc., doesn't make you believe you're in a world that doesn't exist. Doing that would destroy the whole principle of the work. A lot of people make that error; it's the common day event! Just take a look at the masters in this field and you'll see what they do and how they do it. [*Luis Buñuel shoots LOS OLVI-DADOS, his unrelentingly bleak film about juvenile delinquency in Mexico, as if it were a neorealist film. The tension between the realism of the style and the events being depicted create what Freud called "the Uncanny," a major source of horror in literature and film, turning Buñuel's film into a horror film rather than a neorealist exploration of delinquency.*]

★   ★   ★

Let's take a moment and talk about *cinéma vérité* – the documentary genre. Carlos Fuentes, an author from Mexico, was asked about a certain kind of novel – the documentary novels – and he said something which is so true that it is incredible. He said that fiction is documentation. You get more truth out of Dostoyevsky than out of a hundred and fifty thousand documentaries made about Russia. That's the truth!

Why is this the truth? Because an author – in order to say something which may have pertinence to our lives – takes elements from the newspaper, media, etc., and distills them. Shrinks life into an unreal time, which is dramatically real time. I always said, in twenty minutes, you can do the life of a person that lived years. So we can take the time of life and shrink it down to twenty minutes.

That is what our reality is. Not the reality of these people who get together and talk and talk and talk. It is your responsibility to take all this talk and shrink it! That is the authority of the storyteller or filmmaker. Whatever you may call it. But that is also your responsibility because you have our time to deal with. Unless you make home movies. If you make home movies, then the audience is different. Because the audience was in the film! They loved every minute of it when they were acting for us and watching certainly won't be any different.

What I'm objecting to in most documentaries is the people we photograph become actors when you photograph them! They're acting for the camera. You have to reach a point with your camera where your camera will not exist anymore. And that is very difficult to do in documentaries. You ever reach that point with your film?

Fellow: Well, I've spent about two weeks with the
subjects together, and I never saw anything
different than the first day I met them. And
that was a frightening experience.

Vellani: It sounds like you never reached that point,
but you have the responsibility to reach that
point. You know, that's why the documentary is a very difficult genre. Because for most
of the time – even in the ones that I see on
television that are praised – those guys are
acting. You can see acting all over the place.
Reaching the point where they're not acting doesn't take fifteen days. It takes maybe
three months. Or six months.

There was this friend of mine, who was
working for Life magazine, and he invented
a camera that was so silent you didn't know
when you were shooting or you were not
shooting film. He made a documentary
about some drug addicts around New York
City. And he lived with them for more than
six months. He lived with them. And the
amount of footage that was never used is
immense. And the amount of time he spent
with these people – without shooting – was
immense. He kept on going, trying to catch
these people in a moment when they were
not acting. But most of the time they were
still acting, because they sense the presence
of the camera. Even if the camera was not
actually doing anything. They were acting
all the time.

That is why I say this type of filmmaking is rough – it's fake, *cinéma vérité*. Because when you manipulate time, you're gonna manipulate life. We can't change time, but cinema can change time. Therefore, there's nothing true anymore. There's another truth. You see what I mean? The theory of relativity, or a different truth.

The truth is the time. The only time that there is in film is the length of the film, from beginning to end. There is no other. So if it's twenty minutes, we're dealing with twenty minutes. That's the time. That is the real time you're dealing with. Not the time that's described in the events about which the film is made. The events about which the film is made are not the movie. See?

Therefore, you have manipulated reality. So there is no truth anymore. There is something that has to be truth. Truer than truth. The same holds true in life. No matter what you do, no matter what kind of people you deal with, film must be and will only be successful if it reaches an audience as a celebration of life. [*The only film that might be considered a vérité documentary is Andy Warhol's EMPIRE, in which he shoots light as it moves on the Empire State building during twenty-four hours, with no changes in the angle of shooting the light and no editing.*]

The First Ten Minutes

Vellani: The beginning, the first movement, is the crucial part of any film. Forget about the end; if you don't begin the film right, the audience will have left the theatre by the middle. Everything must be precise in the beginning. Donald Sutherland said when he was here that he doesn't like to begin filming a movie with the first scene. You remember why? Because he's not precise, he said. He's not allowed to make any mistakes in the first scene. He'd rather begin shooting a picture in the middle because, as an actor, it takes him time to get the character right. He felt he could be slightly out of character in the middle scenes, but never at the beginning. Remember that. For a filmmaker, that's good advice.

★   ★   ★

If you screw up the first ten minutes of a two-hour film, you have had it. You'll never recuperate. In a short movie, you've got two-and-a-half minutes and that's it. You've got to tell us what kind of picture we're gonna watch!

You have to set your rules and be sure that the audience knows what they are. Never change those rules with the audience. They'll never forgive you.

In RAIDERS OF THE LOST ARK, the rules were set up at the very beginning. People were killed left and right and nobody cared. It was comic book violence – intentionally. The filmmaker let you know immediately that cartoon violence would rule the film.

Within ten minutes of the movie, you know what movie they're gonna make and what its limitations are: "There are things here that are not that real. They're gonna happen, they're gonna be fun." In ten minutes. Zuh-voom. No tricky affair. Throughout the picture you saw that world and they never changed the rules. If in the middle of that movie, they had switched gears into a psychological drama, it would have been a catastrophe. Can't do that. Steven Spielberg set the rules with extraordinary precision. You should study that film very carefully. At the beginning of the film it's set. Bang! And if you don't like this kind of picture, get out right now. Because you're gonna see more of it – only better.

Grab the audience, lead them into it and let them know they're going to a horse race. In the middle, you can be a little wobbly and it doesn't matter. But in the first ten minutes, set the rules of the game and follow them.

★ ★ ★

The tone of a film must be established at the very beginning. This is the responsibility of the filmmaker. You cannot postpone it for a minute. Tell me if the film is a farce. Tell me if it's a comedy. Is it a drama? Is it melodrama? You've got to tell me: I'm ready for anything, but tell me! Otherwise, I'll make up my own mind. And I may be wrong.

The beginning of a film has got to excite our curiosity, you see? "What's gonna happen here?" As soon as you excite the curiosity, then you've got hold of the audience: "Folks, I'm telling this story." See? That's what you must tell me. You must make them feel comfortable. [*Ridley Scott opens ALIEN with a six-minute sequence without dialogue, with the camera taking the audience on a tour of the spaceship Nostromo. When the Alien later starts stalking the crew members, we always know where we are on the spaceship, no matter how fast the camera moves, because of Scott's opening sequence.*]

★　★　★

Have you ever read a Greek tragedy? Plague comes. The messenger says, "My King! Everybody's dying! There's a curse here! You've got to solve it!" The King says, "I'll stop it!" First scene: ZABOOM! You put the old boy in action. The main character. It's then you've got drama.

See? Use the plague! Put the King
in action. Instead of giving me these
information scenes about a character that I
don't know yet. Let him get involved. Let
him lose his job. And then see what he's
made of.

Make me interested to find out who he
is. *Then* tell me about him.

★   ★   ★

At the beginning of ON THE WATER-
FRONT, what do you have? Joey's hanging
out of a window. A man [*Marlon Brando*]
calls: "Joey! Go up to the roof!" Joey gets
there, they throw him off, they kill him.
Next scene – Brando says, "Jesus, I just
thought they were gonna lean on him." In
the first ten minutes – even less – there's a
character who's responsible for a murder and
perhaps did not intend to be. That's what
the story's all about. What is he going to do
about it?

I have said this many times, over
and over again, but: Do not start movies
with information scenes because they
will kill you. When you're writing an
information scene, remember: It will
look like an information scene unless you
have established the conflict prior to that
point. Establish the conflict and then
the information will come as the conflict
develops – and we will get the information

we need to know. Otherwise, the scene will stick up there like raisins in raisin bread. See what I mean? You'll see each one of them.

Get the conflict going! Then you'll get your character in action. After getting the *action* going, *then* you tell me who the actor is. That's when the drama lives.

The Last Ten Minutes

Vellani: I know that in movies they write the words, "THE END," but don't rely upon it. You know? We should feel that the thing is ending, even if you don't use the words, "THE END."

And when that happens, when we are not sure we have reached the conclusion, the audience has not been given enough ingredients to feel the natural course of the play; we do not then reach a catharsis. And we need to feel that, because then we feel something has happened to us. And this is what I think our job is about, to make the audience feel a completion of something.

Fellow: My film doesn't end with an answer.

Vellani: You know that old story about the guy and what is life? He's a middle-aged businessman from New York City, who decides to search for truth and find out what life is, you see? And who knows what life is? Everyone knows that the people who do know are in the Orient. So this guy picks up and goes to India, to the Himalayas, and he talks to this guru, and the guru says, "No, I don't know. This person over there knows." After years and years and years, this guy's clothes are worn out and finally he finds a person who says, "See that mountain over there, way up there, there's an old fella, he knows."

So he climbs up there, through storms, snow, risks his life through all kinds of things, finally, exhausted after all those years, he goes into this cave, and at the end there is this old fella, who says, "Who do you want?"

And the businessman says, "I've come here because I'm told that you have the secret of life."

"I see, you've come to the right place."

And the guy asks, "What is life? Tell me!"

"Life is a bowl of cherries."

"You mean to say I left my business in New York and I've done all these things and after seven years I come in and you tell me that life is a bowl of cherries?"

And the old man says, "Isn't it?"

That's an ending.

Fellow: But I didn't give the answer in the film.

Vellani: You didn't shoot it. You didn't give the answer on purpose. All right. Then you have to give me the answer that you don't have an answer. Like the old man with the bowl of cherries. In other words there is no answer, and that's an answer.

Have you seen Michelangelo Antonioni's BLOW-UP? Do you remember the end of that movie? What does it tell you? What does that ending tell you, with extraordinary clarity? The whole movie is a question of truth, all right? There is a person who is dead, there is a person who is searching for the truth, and at the end, the director tells you, in the movie, what truth is.

Fellow: You mean the truth is…

Vellani: The truth is what you make of it. At the end of the film, some people [*the mimes who appeared at the beginning of the film*] are playing tennis without the ball. But they are playing their hearts out without the ball. [*Even the camera begins to follow the imaginary tennis ball.*] What does the viewer do, the guy watching the ball game?

Fellow: He [*puts down his camera before he*] throws the imaginary ball back at them. Someone hits the ball out, and he throws the ball back at them.

Vellani: He participates, playing also, with his eyes, with the game. And there ain't no ball. This is a major philosophical statement. Pirandello, a playwright writing in the thirties, put forth this very same point of view. So if it pleases you, there is not one truth, there are millions of truths, and one is as true as another. The storyteller must be clear and tell that to the audience. [*And when he picks his camera back up after throwing the imaginary tennis ball back to the mimes, Antonioni erases him from the film.*]

★   ★   ★

A short story usually has an ironic twist at the end that comes like a bombshell. Like the de Maupassant story, "The Necklace." She does all this stuff with the necklace for years and years. At the end, POP! It was a fake! ZAP! That one line really says something, and that's the way the story should be told. So we understand, and the story becomes a comment on life and human nature. De Maupassant has done it with a necklace. And by God, when that line comes in we read it! This woman sacrificed her life for a piece of fake jewelry! Now there is irony! And a telling comment about human behavior. Theatre and film are at their best when showing life that goes so deep. Because they deal then with what we call the celebration of life.

Technique

Camera

Vellani: What we will talk about here is the language of the moving image. When you put an image on the screen, whether it's film or video, the image has to move the audience. The camera that takes that image has got to be on this side or the other side of the scene; it has to take a point of view on the action of the characters in the scene.

The grammar of the visual language is made up of shots. The shots must point out the good things in each scene, the dramatic moments. Don't be afraid of the camera. Don't be terrified of this goddamned machine. Push it around! So you take a bad shot, so what? So many bad shots have been taken that one more is not going to hurt us. Not at all.

★   ★   ★

It is the responsibility of the director in film, as I say over and over again, to photograph the subtext. The camera must score clearly what the subtext of the play is; the text is not enough. The camera must point out with precision what is going on below the text; that's what it should do.

★   ★   ★

Remember, once you've got the scene in mind, you must then decide the dramatic point to be made in the scene. Only then will you know where to put the camera. At that point it becomes a question of common sense. You must show the underlying action of the scene. The responsibility of the film director and the responsibility of the cameraman is to show the subtext. When there is no subtext the camera has nowhere to go. If you just put the camera in a corner and photograph the scenes they become expository.

The scenes become dramatic when you *move the camera*. You must underscore *what* is being said by *how* it is being said. You show *how* with the camera. The line might be said in a close-up; it might be said from across a crowded room; it might be said off camera while the camera shows the reaction of another character in the scene – there are a thousand ways to photograph a line being spoken by an actor, but you must choose the shot that best expresses how that line affects the dramatic content of the scene. The camera has a language all its own – you must learn this visual language, this film grammar to make a good film. [*In THE APARTMENT, Jack Lemmon realizes that Shirley MacLaine has been sleeping with his boss, Fred MacMurray, when she hands him her compact with a broken mirror that she left in Lemmon's apartment. He looks at himself in the cracked mirror, wearing his new bowler hat that signifies his new position on the corporate ladder. The image makes him realize that neither the hat nor the position look good on him. Wilder believed that this shot gave as much information as ten pages of exposition in the screenplay.]*

★ ★ ★

Remember, in filmmaking you must move the camera to different points of view of the action. If you don't do this, if you put the camera in the corner of every scene, you are not a filmmaker. You are a theatre director with a camera in his hands.

Moving the camera does not mean spinning it around the room. You do not move the camera just to see it move. "Look what I can do, look at the camera move, what a shot." Don't move the camera, guide it. Put it where it should be, not where it can be.

I still remember when I was on the set one time with Josh Logan making a film called SAYONARA. The Chapman crane, which had just been invented, arrived on location. And Josh Logan said, "What is that?" as if he didn't know. "It's a Chapman crane, sir." "What does it do – get rid of it." And there went the Chapman crane. Okay? Never to be seen again.

Later on, Logan used the crane, especially in the desert, to move the cameras quicker from set-up to set-up, but never when shooting a scene, never used it to go up and down and sideways. Because Logan knew indiscriminate movement was destructive. Today, there are even more ways to move the camera. And guess what? It's still destructive.

★   ★   ★

The key to making a movie is to make the audience forget that they're watching one. The audience should be interested in the characters. They should feel that what they see is real. They should not be aware that there is a camera, that there is an F-stop, a light meter, any of those things. It bothers me a lot when we see these things, when they are brought in just for effect and not for storytelling purposes. [*Toni summarizes the concept of invisible style in classical Hollywood filmmaking, in the same way Billy Wilder does: "I would like to give the impression that the best directing is the one you don't see. The audience must forget they are in front of a screen - they must be sucked into the screen to the point where they forget the image is only two-dimensional." In other words, if the audience notices a tracking or crane shot, it's distracting them from the characters and the plot.*]

★   ★   ★

You can have a *perfect* film, with photography that is incredible, with one shot that is half in focus or a shaky shot and people will come out of that movie saying, "Terrible photography!" That's exactly what happens. Try to insert a soft focus shot in that Vittorio Storaro movie that was made in China, THE LAST EMPEROR, and you'll see what happens. Because we are *accustomed*, we grow accustomed to a *certain level* of filmmaking. If it's bad photography from beginning to end, pretty soon we forget it and we won't notice. Shaky stuff, cheap sets, we adapt to it and accept it. Because that's the way it is. Be consistent and then the filmmaking will be invisible and nothing will distract us from the story.

★   ★   ★

A word of caution to first-time filmmakers. First-time filmmakers love close-ups. The filmmaking Fellows at AFI have a mania for close-ups. They love talking heads. If I'm from outer space and am told that AFI tapes show examples of what earthlings are, I would imagine that they are people without bodies. I don't know how they move from one room to another; maybe they all have wheelchairs.

Why the constant use of close-up? There's no direction in it, no pleasure in it and very little composition in it. It's an expression. That's it. But it doesn't have any grace; it's an ugly shot. It is used only for psychological emphasis. Not normal. Super-duper normal. Save the close-ups, don't abuse it, so when you need it, you get its power.

★ ★ ★

I just want to point out that when the script asks for close-ups, do not follow those directions literally. You know, I always say if they ask for close-ups, it means there's something missing. Close-ups do not make the story.

Do me a favor, count the close-ups in John Ford's films. Sometimes you find none; sometimes one or two was enough. And yet you understand those stories very well, and they're very moving. So close shots are not the point. The point is: What is the story about? Are the scenes focused correctly? What happens in every scene? You make the point and you get out. Every scene is advancing the story forward. If it doesn't, something is missing. A certain kind of shot will not add emotion that is missing from the story itself. A close-up will not tell you what is in a character's head — only the story can do that.

[*Howard Hawks believed, "When you use close-ups sparingly the public realizes that they are important." He often used medium shots where a less skillful director would use close-ups. John Ford was also famous for his sparing use of close-ups.*]

Sound

Vellani: Music has to tell us what we do not see visually. It has always been that way. From the beginning, in the old 19th century melodramas. That is what "melodrama" means: melody to drama. The good dramatists use music to tell us what we do not see; a great opera would do that.

You understand the psychology of the character through the use of the music. You must establish a meaning for the music. For example, if we have a scene where a young man kisses a young woman, they fall in love, there is a piece of music that is played there. For the remainder of the show that piece of music will mean love. No matter what it is. It could be the national anthem as far as I'm concerned. [*In Otto Preminger's LAURA, David Raksin creates a beautifully haunting love theme that plays as Dana Andrews wanders through the rooms of Laura's apartment searching for some clue to her character and her death. The music and cinematographer Joseph LaShelle's elaborate tracking shots express Andrews' obsession with Laura without using dialogue.*]

In the third act, she leaves. She dies. He thinks. You have this actor who's out there thinking away, you play this piece of music. What is he thinking? The girl. That's how you get tears. That's how drama works. It's a question of establishing memories in the minds of the audience, both sound and visuals. Memories. You establish them. And then you recall them.

I always point out as an example the moment when the woman dies at the end of "Madame Butterfly." Her lover comes in and she's dying and he's arrived too late. What does Puccini play? A love theme! He doesn't play a dirge. *He plays what I don't see.* I see she's dying, so what do I play over her death? *Love,* a dream possibly, and that tears you apart. That is consistent and clear with the premise.

In LA STRADA, after the woman dies, the piece of music that he's playing comes in. Why does Fellini do that? Because after she's dead, you play the music. And underscore his thought process. You see what I'm saying?

That's the use of music. It begins to tell me something, it helps me to apply something that wasn't there before. You have to give music an identity, you see what I'm saying? We use it as a narrative force. [*Listen to the love theme in Bernard Herrmann's score for VERTIGO, in which he musically alludes to Wagner's "Liebestod" in "Tristan and Isolde." When James Stewart kisses Kim Novak on the edge of a cliff above the sea, Herrmann's love theme swells and swells as the waves pound on the cliffs, but we know that their love is inseparable from death.*]

★ ★ ★

It is very tempting for film directors to make comments particularly with music, in their movies. Occasionally, these comments are done with success but it is a very difficult thing to do. Because all of a sudden, if you are a little bit off-center, the audience resents it because your *voice* was there. See? Can't blame the actors, can't blame anything, I blame *you*! Because what you have done is, you have made fun of something that I don't think you should make fun of. This happens all the time in comedies. You see? Musical comments work best when they have already been established with some meaning. The filmmaker's comments, editorials, are just too risky. Stay away from them.

★ ★ ★

I want to talk about sound effects. You know there are some films that are so well made that a telephone *ringing* will tear you apart! Just a little thing like that. But if you start adding other phone calls, and the phone's ringing all the time, nobody cares. So be cautious! Think about every effect you use. Less is more. [*The audience suffers from anxiety in Sergio Leone's ONCE UPON A TIME IN AMER-ICA as a phone rings at least twenty times. Leone finally ends the audience's anxiety when a character answers the call.*]

Editing

Vellani: Film has a tendency to push us around, you
know. You do something, and it's a fight
between the film and yourself. You watch
the screen; every scene wants to be up there
forever. They want to be up there: "Don't
touch me, I want to be on, I want to play!"
The actors want to be up there: "My God, I
want to be on the screen, don't touch me, I
want to be on!"

   Who has the authority? It's a fight between you and that. And you have to find
out very early on who is going to win that
psychological contest. I know the film is going to push you around – are you going to
push it around?

   Then you have a question of the scissors,
right? It's all in your hands. You can cut any
one of the scenes, at any given time. She
does not want to be cut, she does not want
to be altered because she wants every shot to
have its chance. Then finally, you say, "I'll
snip you off."

   Then you have to be very careful, because in this contest, you can't afford to
destroy your opponent. So it's a question of
finessing the situation. It's a deadly contest,
I assure you, deadly. Especially when the
actors are good and the photography's good,
and the shot is great. "I love it, I love it, I
love it," but maybe it doesn't belong on the

screen, maybe it belongs in the paper basket, no matter how good it is. You have to be relentless and absolutely void of any love or desire, you must stop thinking about great moments on the set, because they're absolutely meaningless to an audience.

That scene that you did, the actors were great, the cameraman was great, and you just loved it, but nobody cares. You have to disassociate yourself and look much more objectively at what you're seeing, because otherwise it's going to push you around. Otherwise, the shots will come back at you and you'll think, "Ah, that shot, I'm going to come back to it after the film is over." Somewhere, you are going to see that shot in the picture. You can't do that.

That's a luxury you cannot afford, not when you make films for the public. If you make films for yourself, you can do anything you want. But if it's for yourself and your sister, then you've got to think. Because then you have somebody watching and you can no longer be self-indulgent. [*Joseph LaShelle, the cinematographer of Wilder's THE APARTMENT, was amazed that Wilder didn't shoot protection or coverage. There were no extra close-ups or master shots that could be inserted during the editing, if a producer demanded more coverage: "There was nothing left on the cutting room floor when Wilder was finished."*]

★   ★   ★

When you edit, if you have a scene with
no people in it, think of ways to shorten it,
because "characterless" scenes seem to get
longer and longer and longer. Ten times as
long is the rule of thumb. When you see a
human being in a scene you're much more
patient. With no people on the screen, no
matter how clear it is, the audience will get
bored quickly. [*The antithesis to Toni's classical approach to a scene occurs in Michelangelo
Antonioni's ending for ECLIPSE. We watch a sequence of shots that shows places once inhabited
by the lovers but now are empty. Lasting for seven
minutes, the sequence perfectly ends a film about
fragmented people trying to survive in a fragmented world.*]

★　★　★

Quite often I see overlapping dialogue lines.
But you overlap dialogue at the one moment
where you have established the force; we
must see the actor who speaks – the force
– then you can cut and the force stays with
the overlapping cut. If you don't establish
that force that promotes action, it won't
work because all I get is an action. And the
force becomes very weak because it's not
on the screen. [*Hawks' HIS GIRL FRIDAY thrives
on overlapping dialogue spoken at a rapid pace:
"We wrote the dialogue in a way that made the
beginnings and ends of sentences unnecessary;
they were there for overlapping." In his biography*

of Howard Hawks, Todd McCarthy explains that "Hawks cranked up the pace to where, by one count, the actors were speaking at up to 240 words per minute, compared to the average speaking rate of 100-150..."]

★ ★ ★

In editing, don't forget geography. The audience wants to know where they are in the world of characters. Otherwise, in the middle of the film, when you least expect it, the audience will turn around and say, "Where are we?"

Remember, a scene will play differently in a room with thirty people than in a room with two. Imagine a situation where the characters whisper to each other, telling each other secrets. A room full of people requires whispers. But, if the two people are alone in the room, they don't have to whisper to each other because nobody else is there.

Where people are is critical at all times. It's critical in theatre as well, but more so in film, which does not have the advantage of a fixed stage. Whenever you come to a new situation, you have to remember to tell the audience where you are, where they are, where the actors are. You have to establish the setting of the scene in a master shot, then you can go on to the action of the scene. [*Hitchcock opens PSYCHO with titles that give the audience very specific information: the*

*city where the action will begin, then the exact
date and time. But at the end of the film, Norman
Bates has become his mother and lives in a psychotic state that's beyond time and specificity.]*

The Audience

Vellani: In filmmaking, you must not let the audience get ahead of you. You have to be ahead of them. Filmmaking is a race between the storyteller, who is the screen, and the audience. There's nothing else. It's a race. If you slip once, the race is lost! They've beaten you. Whatever you do in films, you are engaged in a race. You are engaged in a race of understanding between yourself and the audience. The audience is quick, they will draw conclusions constantly. You must stay ahead.

★ ★ ★

You don't want the audience asking questions. In order to keep them from asking questions, you answer the questions before they formulate them. Constantly justify the action of your characters. If you don't, the audience will begin to wonder: "Why does he do such a dumb thing?" You see what I'm saying? Stay ahead of them. Take, for instance, the question of going to the police. These little things bother the hell out of the audience. They really do – why should the characters go to the police? You must make sure in the scene itself that you determine whether it is possible to go to the police. You have a character speak in two or three lines of dialogue: "Some people have gone to the police or have tried to, and it didn't work." So put the lines in the piece, and once you put them in, nobody will argue. When you don't know, say it, then no one asks questions. By having one of the characters say it, you're answering the question before it is asked.

This is something you must do in films all the time – answer the questions before they ask and they'll never ask them. As dumb as they might be, they'll never ask them. [*In PSYCHO, Simon Oakland, a psychiatrist, uses a very simplified version of Freudian ideas to analyze Norman's character. But he answers every major question the audience might ask at the end of PSYCHO in a totally over-the-top performance, as if Hitchcock were telling us not to take this explanation too seriously.*]

You have a story about a group of people on a car trip. The whole story involves what happens in the car on their way from here to San Francisco. You've got to tell the audience why they are going to San Francisco – don't think that it doesn't matter to the story. Tell them, "I'm going to San Francisco to buy a new suit or a hat because they're in a certain store." Whatever it is, tell them! Because if you don't tell them, at the most critical moment the audience will say, "Why the hell are they going to San Francisco anyway?" In order to avoid this sort of thing, lead them; answer the question before they ask it.

★   ★   ★

The first three questions that an audience will ask is: where, when and who? You can't keep the answers a secret from the audience because they're going to ask, and without the answers they're going to be confused. Once you set your stage correctly, then we can begin to see the confrontations between the people or what's at stake.

★   ★   ★

The conflict, as I've said many times, has to be stated very clearly and very early in the piece. You shouldn't waste any time, that's what I recommend. State the conflict. The audience expects it. They want it. Give it to them.

You're in a public house, you've got to please the public. The public wants conflict, that's why they go to the theatre. There's no other reason they go to the theatre. You think they go to the theatre to see everyday life? That's not why they pay money. They go in there because there's something happening with attractive people. If the characters are not attractive enough, the audience doesn't go to the theatre; and if there's not enough going on, they don't stay. [*Robert Zemeckis cast Kurt Russell as Rudy Russo, the unscrupulous head salesman of a dying used car lot, in USED CARS. But no matter how outrageous Rudy's actions are, Russell keeps Rudy likeable because Russell has a likeable persona. The audience goes along with James Stewart's morally dubious actions in REAR WINDOW because of Stewart's all-American persona.*]

★ ★ ★

You have to be able to make people understand what you're saying. Don't keep secrets, not from the audience, because they're going to hate you if you do. And why, why keep secrets? They're nice people. They paid money for seats in the dark to listen to you talk. You've seen the bikinis on the beach these days. And you take me away from that into this room? If you do, it would be nice if you have something to tell me, like whose story it is, and what the person's conflict is. Tell me, then I'll follow. I'll forget the beach.

You'll have control over me, instead of the other way around. You have to keep the narrative force in your hands. The only way to do that is to tell the audience the conflict of the piece and what it's about. Make them curious.

There are two motions that have to happen in the opening of a film — no matter what the film. One, you must make the audience curious so that they lean forward in their seats. Second, you make them lean back in their seats. Do you know what I mean? They are relaxed, and saying, "I'm in good hands."

It is like the dropped shoe. You know? A man one floor above you at the hotel drops a shoe, right past your window. You're awake all night, waiting for the other shoe to fall. That's it. That's what happens in the theatre. If one shoe falls, you've got to drop the other. Don't exploit the audience's curiosity without answering it.

It's not easy to make the audience curious and keep them feeling that they are in good hands, but that's the name of the game, folks. It's very difficult. But when you don't, people get very tired. After a while, they get bored because you lose control of the narrative force.

★　★　★

Get the audience to work. If they don't work mentally they get bored. If it's all done up there for them, they get bored. So the filmmakers are out there, doing their thing, and also criticizing it, tell you what's supposed to happen. And that leaves the audience without a role. So the audience gets bored because they have nothing to do.

Remember, two plus two, never four; give the audience the equation but not the solution. Let them figure it out. [*Hitchcock liked to play with audience expectations because*

*the audience of his TV show knew him as the
"Master of Suspense." In PSYCHO, the audience
came to see a film starring Janet Leigh. The first
third of the film involved them in her story, so
they were completely taken by surprise when the
assumed protagonist was brutally murdered in the
motel shower.*]

Consider life and death. Not the
question of life and death within the play,
but the question of life and death within the
audience. We haven't got much time to stick
around this world, so get on with it. Make
your point and go.

★   ★   ★

Film is a very popular medium. It's supposed
to be. And it's supposed to reach a broad
audience. People haven't gone to Yale and
Harvard. When you use myths in film, that's
fine. But be sure to use a myth that has
reached the status of myth. Napoleon is a
myth. Hitler is a myth. Kennedy is a myth.
Everywhere in the world, people know who
these myths are.

Also, you should realize that if you are
going to paraphrase famous plays, etc.,
for film, do not assume that the audience
is conversant with the action of that play,
because it may not be the case – even if it
is a famous play such as "Hamlet." The
audience is being asked to use a lot of
knowledge that they may not have.

And you can't go there and say:
"You dumb, ignorant people. You don't
understand it." NAH! You're not allowed
to speak. The screen speaks. Therefore, you
better know who you're speaking to and use
things that strike chords so that what you
want to say will come out with clarity. And
then the audience will have no problem
with it.

★   ★   ★

Inappropriate laughs are the enemy of
a dramatic piece. And those have to be
watched out for very, very carefully. I suggest
very strongly that you remember where they
occurred, and try to figure out why.

They occur for many reasons. One,
the audience is embarrassed, and then they
laugh inappropriately. And certain lines
are said, and another story takes place
between the audience and the screen which
has nothing to do with the story the writer
and the director and the cinematographer
photographed. In other words, there is an
undercurrent.

I remember a long time ago, when I was
a young man, there was a movie that was
just about the worst movie that was ever
made, incredible. And what happened is,
it took off. For what it wasn't supposed to
be, and what it was. Word of mouth. This
movie made a fortune. It was a low-budget

film, and earned ten times the money spent
to make it. But the way it played was not
at all what the filmmaker had intended.
There was another movie within the movie
that was very funny, and it had nothing to
do with the story itself. And these types of
situations are very interesting to me because
they have to do with an audience's reaction.
Honest audience reaction.

General

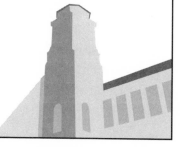

Vellani: Sentiment versus sentimentality; I'm not advising you to avoid sentiment – sentiment makes its way into movies all the way down the line, take a look at John Ford. They play it, boy, and you go for it, but they sometimes mix it with humor to keep the audience where they're supposed to be. They always balance it out.

But when the audience is set up to expect everything, then you risk lapsing into what the audience calls sentimentality. It falls into sentimentality when it becomes "cliché." They will call it cliché because it is cliché, but on the other hand, everything is cliché. ROMEO AND JULIET is full of clichés. One after the other, but they're beautifully done. Clichés are the truth of life, and when done by a great craftsman, all of a sudden, it's beautiful. But to be done well, it must deal with sentiment rather than sentimentality.

When a film becomes too predictable, then the audience will understand it as sentimentality because they don't like to be moved to tears; we don't like to be moved to tears because we then feel that the piece of work invades our privacy. We resent it. If you give us a chance to resent it, we will, and we'll knock it off and say sentimentality.

We don't want to do it, because that's what we don't want. But it's up to you to make us reach that point and to do it carefully and suspenseful enough, with enough truth that we won't be able to reject it. That's the whole trick of sentimental stories or stories with sentiment. [*At the end of THE APART-MENT, when Jack Lemmon starts getting romantic with Shirley MacLaine as they play cards, she tells him, "Shut up and deal." This concluding line keeps the movie from becoming sentimental — it's a happy ending with a great deal of bite.*]

★ ★ ★

All stories are clichés. When we call them soap operas or melodramas or whatever, those are clichés badly made. You've seen copies of OTHELLO, copies of ROMEO AND JULIET, copies of MACBETH that are very badly made. When we watch those, we are not moved. When we see the original, we are moved! And the stories are the same. What's the difference? Remember that William Shakespeare quite often took plays and stories that had already been done before. Same stuff, same scenes, but Shakespeare takes up his pen, starts writing characters and all of a sudden they assume a certain kind of life and we like them. When the others did it, we didn't like them.

So what I'm trying to say is, do not be afraid of emotional pieces. It all depends on how well they're done. I've seen copies of "Death of a Salesman" – hundreds of them. Television is full of them, and they are badly made. But Miller's play is a masterpiece. So it doesn't matter what the story is. It's a question of knowing the craft and the execution of the story.

★   ★   ★

I heard the word "allegory" being used, and I remembered the old saying on Broadway: "Question: what is an allegorical play? Answer: A play that opens on Monday and closes on Tuesday." The theatre is allegorical. The people we invent for the theatre are metaphors. But what we call an allegorical play is a play that we don't understand for some reason or another: where the metaphors that we invented haven't gotten through the barrier to become understandable and reachable to the audience.

We have to make these characters believable from our point of view. That is the whole thrust. And to do that, I always advise not to keep secrets. Authors often think that it is very cute to keep secrets from the audience. I don't know for what purpose. Frankly, there's no merit in keeping secrets from the audience. Because you think you're doing something clever and what you're doing is disturbing folks who paid for their ticket to go there and enjoy themselves

and then they find out that the author wants
to keep slipping off telling the truth about
what he's thinking. So all of a sudden the
guy in the audience says, "Screw you, pal."
That's exactly what's going to happen when
you stretch the elastic a little bit longer. The
elastic that we stretch to create curiosity and
tension can reach only so far. Don't push it
further. By the end of a piece, the audience
must be able to understand what they saw.

★ ★ ★

Sometimes actors "play results," or are told
to "play results." This is wrong. You must
play the action and the result will come
from that process. Quite often, the writer,
in conceiving ideas, plays results. We must
avoid playing results – the results will play
themselves.

Guy de Maupassant used to show his
work to a man called Flaubert. Flaubert read
it, crumpled it up, and put it in a fireplace.
De Maupassant wanted to be a writer
and Flaubert was a famous writer, so de
Maupassant sought his advice. Flaubert told
him something: "We should never cry when
we write. We should cry when we read."
Because if the author cries when he writes
compassionate scenes, nobody is going to
cry when they read them.

If the author is out there and says, "Oh,
my God! Oh, what a scene! It's the most

moving scene I've ever written," it goes down
the drain, I assure you. It's the same thing
as when the actor has a great time – and the
audience sees overacting. Because then what
happens is, the actor does a commentary
about his own acting. And the writer does
a commentary about his own writing. And
the film director does a commentary about
his own directing. [*Toni's approach to acting
resembles that of Hitchcock: "Mostly he is wanted
to behave quietly and naturally (which of course
isn't at all easy), leaving the camera to add most of
the accents and emphases. I would almost say that
the best screen actor is the man who can do nothing
extremely well."*]

★   ★   ★

I like it so much when people don't ham it
up, from both points of view: from in front
of the camera and behind the camera. Both
individuals, the actors and the directors,
have this extraordinary desire to try too
hard. Don't – it's phony and becomes so
mechanical.

★   ★   ★

Do yourself a great favor, don't mess around
with accents. Don't do it. Just play it out.
Do not try to imitate the accents; it doesn't
work! Forget about the regionalism of
Appalachia or wherever you want to set your
story. Because it's phony! You see what I'm

saying? You can't beat it. Take a look at the best work done in the South. There <u>ain't</u> any Southern accents. There <u>ain't</u> any. It's not necessary.

★   ★   ★

In film you should never change costumes unless you really have to. You may want to steal a shot from one scene and put it somewhere else. It's useful if they're wearing the same clothes in each scene.

★   ★   ★

A word about mood in film. Mood is doom spelled backwards. Don't ever forget it. The audience says, "I like the mood of that picture." Think about what they're saying. "Doom" spelled backwards. Because when they talk about mood, photographic mood, they weren't watching what was supposed to be going on in the picture. You know? They were looking at the artifacts, the décor, the colors. What they should be talking about on their way out is the story. Don't confuse pretty pictures with good filmmaking.

★   ★   ★

Don't forget the Chekhov Theory. "If there is a gun hanging on the mantelpiece in the first act, the gun *must go off* in the third act." That's the Chekhov Theory. It must be remembered. [*For Billy Wilder, the three-act structure of a screenplay, reflecting Chekhov and other playwrights who influenced the development of screenplay structure, defined the well-written screenplay: "If you have a problem with the third act, the real problem is in the first act." "The event that occurs at the second-act curtain triggers the end of the movie." "The third act must build, build, build in tempo and action until the last event, and then that's it. Don't hang around."]*

★ ★ ★

Humor is a safety guard of drama. There cannot be drama or tragedy without humor, I assure you. You may get away with it in a twenty-minute piece, but you'll never get away with it in a two-hour piece. Take a look at Shakespeare. That's a lesson in itself. He always has these characters, he brings them in, they do their thing to keep the audience honest. Otherwise, who can take this stuff over and over again? In any film made, you must have it, it's essential to keep the audience going. You've got to have the ups and downs. The great craftsmen in this field are capable of using humor in their films. [*As in Shakespeare's use of the drunken porter in MACBETH.*]

★ ★ ★

Stay away from the front page of newspapers because they date us. They date us terribly. You don't need it, so stay away from it. It's too big. Front page stuff. I'm interested in third page stuff. Just a single individual, like you or me; that's what we care about. That is the nature of things.

★　★　★

Screenplays only have a few moments that are significant. The rest of what's written is there to lead us to those points – to the climaxes, where there's *turnaround*. I was told once that to make a two-hour movie you need *three scenes*. Three scenes that work! That's what we're after. The rest of it is all leading up to those scenes.

★　★　★

Fellow:　Let me ask you a question. Don't you think it gets boring when you tell everything? "This guy is honest. This woman is dishonest. That man is black. This woman is white." That's where films get boring for me.

Vellani:　That's DUMB playwriting. Shakespeare is very clear, and he ain't boring. "Hamlet" is not boring, and I know the premise as it starts. And he tells me, Shakespeare, very clearly that this young man came out of college and went home, and his father was killed under very, very tricky circumstances. Shakespeare. And he's not dumb. And he's not boring. But – he knows the audience. And he tells the audience what this character is all about. That's all I want to know. Not

everybody's Shakespeare, but the rules
are the same: *engage an audience to follow.*
Otherwise, they don't care. And it is the
characterization that will make the audience
care. You have to make part of the story very
clear. And that's not boring, believe me. It
makes the story richer.

We have to put the audience in a
situation where they don't say, "so what?"
To avoid that "so what," you give them an
understanding of the character. Then they
can have compassion for the character.

Take a look at THE BICYCLE THIEF.
De Sica began the film by telling me how
much the bicycle meant to that man!
Cut that scene and the movie is a bore.
The movie doesn't mean anything! If we
don't know that without the bicycle he
cannot feed his family, then you haven't
got anything. "Here's a guy looking for a
bicycle." People say, "Why the hell is he
looking for a bicycle? Big deal, a bicycle."
Nobody cares.

But give me a scene at the head of the
movie where you tell me it's a question of
life and death for that individual to have the
bicycle, that without the bicycle his family's
gonna starve to death. Then follow through
with that man's chase for the bicycle. Then
they'll want him to find that bicycle. That's
what I'm talking about – participation.
Make them care.

Acknowledgments

As we said in our introductions, this book is a collaboration in the best sense of the AFI Conservatory. The letter Gary Winick sent to us in 1992 was from his and Mark Ross' The Acme Company. When we presented the manuscript to Bob Gazzale, AFI's current President, he was immediately supportive. Mark Ross made the book possible, through Gary's estate, with strong endorsements from Gary's other close friends, classmate Carl Franklin (AFI Class of 1986), Niels Mueller and Tobey Maguire. Dean Bob Mandel was involved and committed from day one. And, bringing Jim Hosney onto the team made a huge difference. Toni and Jim were close friends, and Jim had taught Toni's daughter Maria Vellani at Westlake School for Girls, so the intertwining circles were ever-present throughout this project.

Production of this text would not have been possible without Mike Pepin overseeing the multiple editions and headaches that come with every publication. And, Howell Begle has been AFI's legal advisor since our first days. We asked a few others to tell us if we were going in the right direction, and Josh Kushins, Abraham Tetenbaum and Lynn Roth were deeply caring in their comments. Richard Bontems and Pat Hanson were especially helpful in the final preparation of the manuscript. By chance, we met Jeffrey Goldman, and his publishing expertise became central to our progress. Thanks especially to Amy Inouye and her Future Studio.

More months ago than I care to admit, I told one of my grandchildren that I was publishing a book. She screamed with excitement, "Granny J, you're writing a book!" Not exactly, I explained, but Jamie and I are working together again to get a book published. It has been so much fun, and it is a proud moment for the two of us to be associated again to further the legacy of the AFI and the AFI Conservatory.

JPF & JH

BIOGRAPHY
Toni Vellani

Antonio Vellani was born and raised in Bologna, Italy, where he studied law. He came to the United States in his mid-twenties, studied film and learned film production in documentary, and in 1959 he started working in Los Angeles as an associate producer for George Stevens, Sr. In 1965 he was appointed head of the Documentary Film Division at the U.S. Information Agency in Washington, DC. He returned to Los Angeles and began his relationship with AFI in 1968 as Production Coordinator for AFI's Center for Advanced Film Studies (which became the AFI Conservatory in 2000) and served as its Director for more than a decade through the force of his intellect and the power of his personality.

At Toni's Memorial Service, director Bob Mandel, AFI Class of 1977, best summarized Vellani's essence:

"Just as any great institution takes on the character of its leader, Bob Brustein at Yale, John Houseman at Juilliard, so did AFI for many years take on the spirit and humanity of Toni Vellani."

(Mandel went on to emulate his Master Teacher by being named Dean of the AFI Conservatory in 2005.)

BIOGRAPHY

Gary Winick

A New Yorker, Gary Winick spent his student years earning a BA from Tufts University and two Masters of Fine Arts: from the University of Texas, Austin, and the American Film Institute.

He started his filmmaking career as a producer-director on low-budget, direct-to-video projects, but gradually segued into directing, finding his greatest strength creatively collaborating with colleagues and actors in the service of telling stories.

In 1999, Winick built the all-digital production company InDigEnt which introduced the indie community to inexpensive new technology, making films at an unheard-of benchmark of $100,000. At this time it was a new idea – a smart idea – that prefigured the digital revolution soon to come.

> Movies produced through InDigEnt included:
> Winick's TADPOLE
> Richard Linklater's TAPE
> Rebecca Miller's PERSONAL VELOCITY
> Peter Hedges' PIECES OF APRIL, in which
> Patricia Clarkson was nominated for an Oscar.

Winick then turned to the Hollywood feature and, just as in every genre he took on, he mastered its structure to tell personal stories that resonated across generations, including:

13 GOING ON 30
CHARLOTTE'S WEB
BRIDE WARS
LETTERS TO JULIET

Winick received numerous awards including:
Sundance Best Director (TADPOLE)
AFI Franklin J. Schaffner Alumni Medal in 2007

BIOGRAPHY
Bob Gazzale

B ob Gazzale became AFI's third President and CEO in November 2007. Gazzale joined the Institute in 1992 and has held various positions, including Director, AFI National Programs, in New York and Director, AFI Productions, in Los Angeles. He has served as writer and executive producer of the AFI Life Achievement Award telecasts since 2001, and was a principal in the team that created, produced and wrote the **AFI's 100 YEARS...** series, which has driven millions of people back to the classics of American film. He also created the format for AFI Awards, the Institute's annual almanac of excellence, as well as the popular "AFI Night at the Movies."

Gazzale is a graduate of the University of Virginia, where he helped launch the Virginia Festival of American film in 1988. Gazzale served as Director of the festival until he joined AFI.

BIOGRAPHY
Jean Picker Firstenberg

Jean Picker Firstenberg retired after almost 28 years as President and CEO of AFI in late October 2007. Her tenure marked AFI as one of America's great national cultural and educational resources. In addition, AFI's role in celebrating and recognizing excellence in America's film, television and digital media has been acknowledged worldwide. Her retirement came at the conclusion of AFI's 40th Anniversary celebration where she was presented an AFI Life Achievement Award for service to the Institute. She was named President Emerita and a Lifetime Trustee.

Firstenberg's impact on AFI began in 1980, when the Institute acquired an eight-acre campus in Los Angeles. She led AFI through many other significant advancements, ranging from the AFI Conservatory being accredited by both the National Association of Schools of Art and Design, and the Accrediting Commission for Senior Colleges and Universities of the Western Association of Schools and Colleges, to the opening of the AFI Silver Theatre and Cultural Center – a state-of-the-art center for the moving image arts in Silver Spring, Maryland – to AFI FEST (AFI Los Angeles International Film Festival), the success of which over 27 years has helped make AFI the largest nonprofit exhibitor in the U.S. Under Firstenberg's leadership, AFI transitioned from a grants-dependent organization to a leading entrepreneurial nonprofit of the 21st century, having expanded AFI's national programs and outreach to include television, video and digital media.

Firstenberg is a summa cum laude graduate of Boston University's College of Communications. She has been a member of several boards and received many honors in the world of film and television.

BIOGRAPHY
James Hindman

J ames Hindman's career has focused on the arts, education and public programs; he has developed large-scale educational programs, festivals and exhibition venues in the United States, the Middle East and Asia.

Hindman held senior positions at AFI from 1981-2004, including Co-Director and COO from 1996-2004. He oversaw an annual budget of $25 million and an Institute staff of 150 in Los Angeles and Washington, DC. He also served as Provost of the AFI Conservatory, helping to secure its formal accreditation as an independent graduate school. He was Executive Producer for the critically acclaimed AFI feature documentary, VISIONS OF LIGHT, and developed the national documentary festival Silverdocs for AFI, now known as AFI DOCS.

Since leaving AFI, Hindman's major projects include the launching of two new film schools, designing both the curriculum and the facilities of the Creative Media Institute at New Mexico State University, Las Cruces, and the innovative graduate program for the Red Sea Institute of Cinematic Arts in Jordan.

Prior to joining AFI, Hindman served as professor and Director of Theater at American University in Washington, DC. He holds a Ph.D. in Drama from the

University of Georgia, an MA in Speech and Theater from the University of Maryland and a BA in Speech and Theater from Loyola University, Chicago.

BIOGRAPHY

Jim Hosney

Recognized as a prominent film historian, Hosney has devoted his life to education. He has taught at the AFI Conservatory for close to 40 years; he is currently the Distinguished Scholar-in-Residence, teaches a class in American Film for First Year Fellows and moderates the Harold Lloyd Master Seminar series.

At the Westlake School for Girls in Los Angeles, Hosney taught film, literature and American Studies for ten years; at Crossroads School for the Arts and Sciences in Santa Monica, he was director of the Film and Video Program and the Great Books Honors English Program for 25 years. Hosney is a graduate of Occidental College, where he majored in Anglo-American Literature.

OBITUARY

Gary Winick

Written by RYAN GILBEY
Originally published in The Guardian – March 2, 2011.
Copyright Guardian News & Media Ltd 2011.

The director and producer Gary Winick, who has died of brain cancer aged 49, was at the forefront of American cinema's adoption of digital video (DV), along with more high-profile names such as Steven Soderbergh and David Fincher. Winick believed that the discreet, lightweight equipment involved, and the flexibility it afforded film-makers, could lead to more direct and emotionally authentic movies, citing "the intimacy that occurs with the actors because of the small cameras". His own work, notably the 2002 coming-of-age story Tadpole, provided some persuasive evidence. His DV-oriented production company, InDigEnt (Indpendent Digital Entertainment), gave others the funds and encouragement to experiment for themselves. While he insisted on preparation and professionalism ("Don't think that going digital means you can just 'wing it'," he advised newcomers), spontaneity lay at the heart of his approach: "One of the things I always say is: you just gotta go out and do it, you can't wait for the right time. Nine times out of 10 if you just go out and do it, good things will happen."

He was born in New York City to Alan and Penny Winick. He graduated from Tufts University, Massachusetts, in 1984, before gaining degrees from the University of Texas at Austin and the American Film Institute, Los Angeles. In 1986 he edited Carl Franklin's short film Punk before writing and directing five features of his own which gave him experience but brought scant attention. Curfew (1989) and Out of the Rain (1991) were little-seen thrillers, the former so violent that it suffered censorship and certification problems in the UK.

His subsequent movies hinted at a more contemplative sensibility that would emerge in his later work. Sweet Nothing (1995), The Tic Code (1999) and Sam the Man (2001) – films which tackled, respectively, crack addiction, Tourette syndrome and the life of a blocked, adulterous novelist – had their defenders among critics, but never found an audience in the crowded marketplace of independent cinema.

By the late 1990s, Winick had caught a glimpse of the digital dawn, and felt invigorated by what he saw. While The Tic Code languished on the shelf awaiting a distributor, Winick went with its cinematographer, Wolfgang Held, to see Thomas Vinterberg's international success Festen (The Celebration). This 1998 drama adhered to the purist stipulations of the Dogme 95 manifesto that Vinterberg had drawn up with three fellow Danish directors, and was shot entirely on DV.

"After the movie ended we couldn't stop talking about how wonderful it was," Winick recalled, "and how liberating digital video must be. We thought about how John Cassavetes worked in the 1960s and 1970s.

His films were all about truth of character and setting, and we thought that if he were around now, he'd probably be a big fan of DV. The collaboration Cassavetes had with his actors, the moments he found, were so intimate and truthful. Digital video lends itself to that perfectly."

Winick launched the New York-based InDigEnt in 1999 with financing from the Independent Film Channel and an agreement to produce 10 digital features on minimal budgets. "I wanted this movement to be like the French New Wave," he said, "in which directors told different types of stories and used the language of cinema a little differently, with smaller cameras on real locations."

Early fruits included Richard Linklater's tense chamber-piece Tape (2001), and debut films from actors-turned-directors – The Anniversary Party (2001), which starred its writer-producer-director team, Jennifer Jason Leigh and Alan Cumming, and Ethan Hawke's Chelsea Walls (2002), with Uma Thurman and Kris Kristofferson. The films faced accusations of self-indulgence, but Winick considered The Anniversary Party in particular to be a turning point because "it was the first film where you had movie stars in a DV film, and I think audiences really didn't distinguish between DV and 35mm".

Winick's own first film under the InDigEnt banner testified to the commercial and artistic potential of DV for US audiences. Made for just $150,000, Tadpole was a Graduate-inspired comedy about a self-consciously intellectual, Voltaire-quoting 15-year-old (Aaron Stanford) yearning after his stepmother (Sigourney

Weaver) while also involved with her best friend (Bebe
Neuwirth). Its premiere in competition at the 2002
Sundance film festival was followed by a best director
prize for Winick and a $5m acquisition by the distribu-
tor Miramax. (Less remarked upon was InDigEnt's bold
profit-sharing structure, which ensured that Tadpole's
crewmembers received substantial payouts.) It was a
banner year for InDigEnt at Sundance for another reason: Rebecca Miller's Personal Velocity, also produced
by the company, won two awards including the coveted
grand jury prize. In 2003, InDigEnt's drama Pieces of
April earned an Oscar nomination for one of its stars,
Patricia Clarkson.

By this time, Winick was moving into the mainstream. His light touch and evident compassion made
13 Going On 30 (2004), starring Jennifer Garner as an
adolescent who wakes up in an adult body, better than
the average popcorn romcom. Nevertheless, he was
perturbed by the sudden rise in production costs rep-
resented by the new film's multi-million-dollar budget.
"It is incredible when you look at the excess money on
a big-scale production such as 13 Going On 30," he
reflected. "I said to [the film's producer] Joe Roth, 'You
know, you could make 111 InDigEnt films for one 13
Going On 30' and he said, 'Yeah but 111 InDigEnt
films wouldn't make as much money as one 13 Going
On 30.' It is big business and they've worked it out and
although they have excess money and it feels wasteful to
me, it obviously is not to them."

The remainder of Winick's career was devoted to
movies aimed squarely at the multiplexes. He made an
effects-laden, live-action adaptation of EB White's chil-

dren's novel Charlotte's Web (2006), with a voice cast headed by Julia Roberts, and the comedy Bride Wars (2009), starring Anne Hathaway and Kate Hudson. His last film, completed after undergoing surgery for brain cancer, was the romantic road movie Letters to Juliet (2010).

InDigEnt continued to back unorthodox projects, such as the award-winning Starting Out in the Evening (2007) and Steve Buscemi's dark comedy Lonesome Jim (2005). Box-office rewards proved sporadic. "I think we are pushing the medium," Winick said. "But is it out there in the mainstream? Not yet, because obviously these stories unfortunately don't lend themselves to a big market. But I think for film-makers and people who go to films and want to see something different, we have definitely achieved that goal."

Gary Scott Winick,
film producer and director,
born 31 March 1961; died 27 February 2011